IS FEENEYISM CATHOLIC?

The Catholic Meaning of the Dogma,
"Outside the Catholic Church
There Is No Salvation"

REV. FR. FRANÇOIS LAISNEY

ANGELUS PRESS
2918 TRACY AVENUE, KANSAS CITY, MISSOURI 64109

On the cover: Fr. Leonard Feeney

Library of Congress Cataloging-in-Publication Data

Laisney, François, 1957-
   Is Feeneyism Catholic? / François Laisney.
   p. cm.
   Rev. ed. of. Baptism of desire. c1991.
   Includes bibliographical references and index.
   ISBN 1-892331-04-7
     1. Salvation outside the Catholic Church. 2. Feeney, Leonard, 1897-1978. 3. Baptism--Catholic Church. I. Laisney, François, 1957- Baptism of desire. II. Title.

BT755 .L37 2001
234--dc21   2001035290

©2001 by Angelus Press
All rights reserved. No part of this book may be reproduced or transmitted in any form or by any means, electronic or mechanical, including photocopying, recording, or by any information storage and retrieval systems without permission in writing from the publisher, except by a reviewer, who may quote brief passages in a review.

ANGELUS PRESS
2918 TRACY AVENUE
KANSAS CITY, MISSOURI 64109
PHONE (816) 753-3150
FAX (816) 753-3557
ORDER LINE 1-800-966-7337

ISBN 1-892331-04-7
FIRST PRINTING—January 1991
SECOND EDITION—June 2001

Printed in the United States of America

To Our Lady, Guardian of the Faith,
Mother of Mercy,
Whose prayers for the salvation
of souls are always answered.

To the Bishop who taught me the Faith, who
"has given us what he received"
(I Cor. 15:3),
And who "in time of wrath, was made a
reconciliation" (Ecclus. 44:17).

Contents

Introduction to the Second Edition 1

Introduction to the First Edition 5

Exposition of the Doctrine 7
    There Is a Law Established by Jesus Christ, That Every Man
        Must Be Baptized in Order to Be Saved 7
    God Is Not Bound by the Laws He Has Set 7
    God Does Sometimes Work Such Miracles 8
    One Who Has Received Sanctifying Grace
        Before the Actual Reception of the Sacrament
        Is Not Dispensed from the Law of God,
        Obliging Him to Receive the Sacrament 8
    It May and Did Happen That Some Died
        Before They Could Fulfill This Good Will,
        and "God Counts the Will for the Fact" 9
    "Baptism of Desire" Is Not a Sacrament;
        It Does Not Have the Exterior Sign
        Required in the Sacraments 9
    One Must Insist Upon the Fact That
        the Interior Sanctifying Grace, with the Virtues
        of Catholic Faith, Hope and Charity,
        Is Absolutely Necessary for Salvation 10
    One Direct Consequence of What Has Been Said
        So Far Is That These Souls Belong
        to the Mystical Body of Christ,
        Which Is the Catholic Church 12
    How Does One Receive This Sanctifying Grace? 12

Some Liberal Errors 15
    Does Sincerity with Ignorance Save? 15
    What About the "Good Heathen"? 16
    Is Baptism of Desire Very Common? 18
    Faith Entirely Implicit? 20
    "I Was Hungry…" 24

Contents

The Roots of the Liberal Errors 26
If God Is So Good, How Can He
    Let All These Pagans Be Damned? 27

THE TEACHING OF THE CHURCH ON BAPTISM OF BLOOD AND BAPTISM OF DESIRE 31

OVERVIEW 31
THE AUTHORITY OF THE SCRIPTURES 33
    John 3:5 33
    Is John 3:5 a Law? 36
    A Scriptural Lesson on St. John by St. Thomas Aquinas 37
    The Scriptures Teach Baptism
        of Blood and Baptism of Desire 40
THE AUTHORITY OF POPES AND COUNCILS 42
    Innocent III and the Fourth Lateran Council 42
    Boniface VIII: *Unam Sanctam* 44
    Eugene IV and the Council of Florence 45
    Council of Trent 49
    Pius IX 51
    St. Pius X 53
    Benedict XV 54
THE AUTHORITY OF THE FATHERS 54
    The Roman Martyrology 54
    Fathers on Baptism of Blood 56
    St. Cyprian (3rd century) 57
    St. Ambrose (3rd century) 61
    St. Augustine (4th century) 62
    St. Gregory Nazianzen 64
THE AUTHORITY OF DOCTORS 67
    St. Bernard 67
    St. Albert the Great 69
    St. Bonaventure 69
    St. Thomas Aquinas 69
    St. Robert Bellarmine 75
    St. Alphonsus Liguori 77
THE AUTHORITY OF OTHER SAINTS OR THEOLOGIANS 78
    Catechism of the Council of Trent 78
    Holy Mystics 78

Theologians 78
Bishop George Hay 81
Fr. Michael Müller, C.Ss.R. 81
Orestes Brownson 83
Two Typical Examples of Baptism of Desire 84
CONCLUSION: *EODEM SENSU, EADEMQUE SENTENTIA* 85
The Dilemma 88

ANSWER TO ADDITIONAL OBJECTIONS OF FR. FEENEY 91

The Precise Error of Fr. Feeney 91
Do Not Confuse Sanctifying Grace and Character 92
Justification and Salvation 98
Unfulfilled and Fulfilled Justice 101
Were Some Miracles Performed
 to Prove the Necessity of Baptism of Water? 103
Necessity of the Magisterium of the Church 104
What is the Necessity of the
 Exterior Belonging to the Church? 105
Is There a Loophole? 108
The Fundamental Error of Fr. Feeney 110
Can Fr. Feeney and His Followers
 Be Called "Heretics"? 112
What About the Letter of the Holy Office
 to Cardinal Cushing (July 27, 1949)? 112
CONCLUSION 115

APPENDIX I
THEOLOGIANS 117

INTRODUCTION TO THE SECOND EDITION

"We have known and have believed the charity[1] which God hath to us. God is charity: and he that abideth in charity abideth in God, and God in him" (I Jn. 4:16). This charity of God for us is wholly summed up in the mystery of the Church: the most Holy Trinity calls us to be partakers of the Divine Life, by becoming members of the Mystical Body of the incarnate Word of God, Our Lord Jesus Christ. The true Church is more than just a place where we find the true doctrine of Our Lord Jesus Christ, His sacraments and all the means of salvation; it is the very place where alone we can live of the life of God in Jesus Christ Our Lord. It is the Mystical Body of Christ.

That there is only one true Church, the One, Holy, Catholic, Apostolic, and Roman Church, outside of which no one can be saved, has always been taught by the Catholic Church. This dogma, however, has been under attack in recent times. Already last century, the popes[2] had to repeatedly rebuke the liberal Catholics for their tendency to dilute this dogma, "reducing it to a meaningless formula."[3] But in the late 1940's and early 1950's, the same dogma has been misrepresented on the opposite side by Fr. Feeney and his followers, changing "outside the Church there is no salvation" into "without water baptism there is absolutely no salvation," thereby denying doctrines which had been positively and unanimously taught by the Church, *viz.* Baptism of Blood and Baptism of Desire.

What is at stake? *Fidelity to the unchangeable Catholic Faith, to the Tradition of the Church.* We must neither deviate on the left

---

[1] *Credidimus caritati*, this was the motto of Archbishop Lefebvre.
[2] Pope Pius IX, in *The Sources of Catholic Dogma* [hereafter Dz.], tr. by Roy J Defarrari from the 30th edition of Henry Denzinger's *Enchiridion Symbolourm*, (St. Louis, MO: B. Herder Book Co., 1957) 1646-1648, 1677, *etc.*
[3] Pope Pius XII, *Humani Generis.*

nor on the right. The teaching Church must "religiously guard and faithfully explain the deposit of Faith that was handed down through the Apostles,...this apostolic doctrine that all the Fathers held, and the holy orthodox Doctors reverenced and followed" (Vatican I, Dz. 1836); all members of the Church must receive that same doctrine, without picking and choosing what they will believe. We may not deny a point of doctrine that belongs to the deposit of Faith–though not yet defined–under the pretext that it has been distorted by the Liberals.

Moreover, there is at stake a whole attitude of mind in front of the truth of Faith. The Catholic Church teaches that Faith is the adhesion of the intelligence to the truth revealed by God, Who can neither deceive nor be deceived, which truth is faithfully taught by the Catholic Church. Faith therefore is *a humble reception of Truth*, a submission of the intelligence. This Catholic attitude of the faithful is called by St. Paul "the obedience of Faith" (Rom. 1:5, 16:26, Acts 6:7). Hence, when one sees so many holy Fathers, holy doctors, popes, saints and approved theologians teach as unanimously a doctrine as this one, the proper Catholic attitude is to *receive* it with docility, striving to understand it "in the same sense and in the same words."[4] It is not a Catholic attitude to reject one point of Faith, under the pretext of holding fast to another point of Faith, pretending that they are incompatible. The compatibility between both has been taught from the beginning, and wonderfully explained by the Doctors; it is not Catholic to reject the Doctors' doctrine, claiming to "improve upon the teaching of some of the Doctors."[5]

This book was first printed by Angelus Press with the title: *Baptism of Desire*. This second edition has been so deeply reworked that it could be fairly called a new book(!), though the whole material of the first edition is still found here. More research has been done for it, more Doctors and theologians have been consulted, all of them being found in perfect agreement with the traditional doctrine. I want to thank especially Fr. Joseph Pfeiffer and Mrs. Mary Buckalew for their research on this matter, which proved invaluable.

---

[4] *Eodem sensu eademque sententia*, I Cor. 1:10, quoted by Vatican I, Dz. 1800.
[5] Brother Michael, letter of March 3, 1986.

Introduction to the Second Edition

The doctrine presented in this book, dear reader, is not mine, "it is that which I have received, which I pass on to you" (I Cor. 11:23, 15:3), it is the age-old doctrine of the Catholic Church. One can see the divine Providence in the struggle of the Society of Saint Pius X to uphold the doctrine of the Fathers against the followers of Fr. Feeney. Indeed, the great crisis of the Church is indubitably a crisis of fidelity to Tradition. The authority of the Church is not above the deposit of Faith; authority has been given by Our Lord to Peter and the Apostles in the service of the Truth; its duty is to uphold it and to pass it on, not to change it to fit the modern world. Fighting against the novelties introduced by the Second Vatican Council on the liberal side, the Society of Saint Pius X has been accused of following their own private judgment. The occasion of this struggle against the followers of Fr. Feeney manifests that the rule we follow is the rule of Faith given by Tradition; we do not change an iota. We simply want to be faithful to the Church's unchangeable teaching, not following our own judgment, but holding fast to that which has been handed down to us by the Church.

May St. Pius X help us to remain faithful, and may all these holy doctors, whose doctrine we defend, give every reader of this book the light and love to humbly receive their doctrine, in order to go to heaven with them. O Mary, Seat of Wisdom, pray for us!

Rev. Fr. François Laisney

INTRODUCTION TO THE FIRST EDITION

This little study can be summarized in one very simple truth of our catechism: *in order to go to heaven, one must die in the state of grace.* That grace is given to us only *through Jesus Christ and with Jesus Christ and in Jesus Christ, i.e.,* in His Church, chiefly through the sacraments.

This Catholic doctrine has been watered down by some Liberals who have practically reduced to very little the necessity of the sacraments and of belonging to the Catholic Church, "outside of which there is no salvation," and have even sometimes reduced the necessity of grace itself, replacing it by "invincible ignorance and sincerity."

On the other hand, Fr. Feeney over-reacted against them and said that the state of grace was not sufficient for salvation, making the character of baptism an absolute necessity, hereby teaching novelty. He put too much emphasis on the exterior belonging to the Church, while the Fathers, Doctors and popes have always put the emphasis on the interior bond with Christ, "Charity, which is the bond of perfection" (Col. 3:14).

I hope and pray that the consideration of the Catholic Truth will help you, dear reader, to appreciate more the necessity and value of the interior life of Christ in us by Catholic faith and charity–a true beginning of the life of heaven–and to be enkindled to communicate this treasure to many other souls, because without this life of grace, by which we are living members of the Catholic Church, there is no salvation, even if one belongs to the Church.

In order to walk on sure ground, the question has been approached from the point of view of grace. Indeed the doctrine on grace has been well and precisely defined by the Church, so that all Catholics interested in the question of baptism of desire adhere to these truths, which therefore provide a solid and non-controversial approach.

Our Lord Jesus Christ did not come to condone evil, nor to condemn the sinner, but rather to save the sinners from their sins:

> For God so loved the world, as to give His only begotten Son; that whosoever believeth in Him, may not perish, but may have life everlasting. For God sent not his Son into the world, to judge the world, but that the world may be saved by Him (Jn. 3:16, 17).

It is therefore the mission of the Church neither to condone evil, nor to condemn the sinner, but to save the sinners from their sins, through a living faith in Jesus Christ.

Through the intercession of the Immaculate Heart of Mary and of St. Theresa, Patron of the Missions, may the Sacred Heart enkindle this missionary charity in the souls of our readers and in ours!

May we also "receive the love of the Truth," without which we would become the prey of "the operation of error, to believe lying: that all may be judged who have not believed the truth, but have consented to iniquity" (II Thess. 2:10, 11).

Rev. Fr. François Laisney

EXPOSITION OF THE DOCTRINE

THERE IS A LAW[6] ESTABLISHED BY JESUS CHRIST, THAT EVERY MAN MUST BE BAPTIZED IN ORDER TO BE SAVED

"Amen, amen I say to thee, unless a man be born again of water and the Holy Ghost, he cannot enter into the kingdom of God" (Jn. 3:5).[7] Our Lord clearly speaks here of the sacrament of baptism, *i.e.,* the baptism of water. The Council of Trent teaches that the sacrament of baptism is the "instrumental cause" of grace in the soul: it is the ordinary and obligatory means of receiving the grace of God for the first time.

This law does not establish a mere extrinsic necessity of baptism; like the laws of nature, it belongs to the very nature of baptism to cause grace in our souls (*ex opere operato*): for the unbaptized, it is the only means at his disposal to get this grace.

GOD IS NOT BOUND BY THE LAWS HE HAS SET

In the natural order God sometimes produces an effect bypassing the ordinary secondary causes He has established: this is called "a miracle." In a similar way also, He sometimes produces grace in souls bypassing the ordinary secondary causes, *i.e.,* without the exterior sign of the sacrament: this is like a miracle in the supernatural order. For example, when Christ walked on the waters He produced an effect (to support His body above the water) without the natural cause (a solid ground), thus not following the law of gravity. In the same way, He can give His grace and thus open heaven to a soul without the waters of baptism.

Hence the definition of Baptism of Desire by St. Thomas Aquinas:

> Forasmuch as someone's heart is moved by the Holy Ghost to believe in and love God and to repent of his sins, not only

---

[6] See p.36 why it is a law.
[7] For a more complete explanation of these words of Our Lord Jesus Christ, see p.33.

without Baptism of Water, but also without Baptism of Blood, one receives the effect of Baptism by the power of the Holy Ghost (*Summa Theologica,* [hereafter *ST*] III, Q.66 A.11).

The same is true after baptism. If one loses sanctifying grace by a mortal sin, he ought to go to confession, repent for his sins, accuse them to the priest, receive the absolution and do the penance given by the priest. Yet, God can restore sanctifying grace in this soul even before the actual reception of the sacrament of Confession, by the soul's act of perfect contrition: perfect contrition is for the sacrament of penance what baptism of desire is for the sacrament of baptism.

GOD DOES SOMETIMES WORK SUCH MIRACLES

That some receive sanctifying grace before baptism of water is not only a possibility, it is a fact! St. Augustine speaks of Catholic catechumens "burning with charity," giving the example of the Centurion Cornelius (Acts 10:44,47) who was "filled with the Holy Ghost before his baptism."[8]

ONE WHO HAS RECEIVED SANCTIFYING GRACE BEFORE THE ACTUAL RECEPTION OF THE SACRAMENT IS NOT DISPENSED FROM THE LAW OF GOD, OBLIGING HIM TO RECEIVE THE SACRAMENT

This law still applies to him. As a matter of fact, he would not have the grace of God unless his will were submissive to the Will of God, thus including (implicitly or explicitly) the will to receive the sacrament. This is true of baptism of desire. It is true also of perfect contrition: it does not dispense from confession, it cannot even be had without the will to go to confession as soon as possible.

It is important to stress here that baptism of desire is more than the mere desire of baptism, in a similar way that perfect contrition is more than the mere desire of confession. In both cases, the former includes the full spiritual life (sanctifying grace with a "living faith," "working through charity," with detestation of all

---

[8] *De Baptismo,* 4, 21, 28, Rouët de Journel, *Enchiridion Patristicum,* No.1629 (henceforth referenced as "R.J.").

past sins for the love of God), the latter can be the effect of a mere actual grace.

In both cases too, if one fully co-operates with actual grace, Jesus Christ will lead this soul to the fullness of His spiritual life, because the goal and end of actual grace is always the gift of sanctifying grace.

IT MAY AND DID HAPPEN THAT SOME DIED BEFORE THEY COULD FULFILL THIS GOOD WILL, AND "GOD COUNTS THE WILL FOR THE FACT"[9]

God does not ask the impossible. If, without fault on one's part, such a person with baptism of desire (or perfect contrition) is prevented from the exterior reception of the sacrament before his death, he can still go to heaven. This fact of baptism of desire is undeniable. It is a truth solidly established in the history of the Church and asserted in the writings of the saints and popes (see references p.54) that God did and does save souls, giving them His grace (the interior grace of baptism) without the sacrament (exterior sign) of baptism. At the beginning of the Church the most obvious such case was when a Catholic catechumen would die martyr before receiving the water of Baptism: this is Baptism of Blood, which–the Church teaches–can save also little children dying with their parents for Christ.

"BAPTISM OF DESIRE" IS NOT A SACRAMENT; IT DOES NOT HAVE THE EXTERIOR SIGN REQUIRED IN THE SACRAMENTS[10]

The theologians, following St. Thomas Aquinas, prince of theologians, call it "baptism" only because it produces the grace of baptism, the new birth, which is the most important thing in baptism; yet it does not produce the sacramental character. St. Thomas calls it "baptism of the Spirit," because it is the Holy Ghost giving the light of faith and burning love of charity in the soul.

Note also that baptism of blood, according to St. Cyprian, St. Thomas, *etc.*, is even more perfect than baptism of water, because

---

[9] *ST*, III, Q.68, A.2, ad 3.
[10] *Ibid.*, III, Q.66, A.11, ad 2.

of the greater conformity with Our Lord Jesus Christ crucified, source of all graces. Hence baptism of blood not only washes away all the punishment due to sin as does baptism of water, but also gives a fullness of merit and a special crown! All the Doctors have taught that martyrdom leads directly to heaven!

However, baptism of desire (more probably) does not wash away all the punishment due to sin. Thus after baptism of desire, one might still have to pass through purgatory. Pope Innocent III ordered prayers and sacrifices for such souls.[11] St. Thomas teaches this explicitly in his *Summa Theologica* (III, Q.68, A.2, ad 2).

ONE MUST INSIST UPON THE FACT THAT THE INTERIOR SANCTIFYING GRACE, WITH THE VIRTUES OF CATHOLIC FAITH, HOPE AND CHARITY, IS ABSOLUTELY NECESSARY FOR SALVATION

The very nature of baptism of desire is the direct infusion of sanctifying grace, with the supernatural virtues, faith, hope and charity, in the soul by God. Therefore, if anyone denies any truth of the Catholic Faith, he does not have baptism of desire, and he cannot go to heaven, unless he repents from this denial.

Sanctifying grace is not "a means of salvation" (like a replaceable tool), it is the very constitutive element of the adoption as children of God. It is a "participation of the Divine Nature" (II Pet. 1:4). Charity is by its very nature a friendship with God. The Church has always taught that there is no remission of sin without the infusion of sanctifying grace.[12] St. Paul is clear: "Without faith it is impossible to please God" (Heb. 11:6). He speaks of the true Faith, of course! He also wrote that God "wants all men to be saved and to come to the knowledge of the truth" (I Tim. 2:4); thus salvation cannot be attained by one with the use of his reason alone, without God revealing and man believing this truth by a supernatural virtue and an act of faith. He does not have to know everything explicitly, but he has to believe explicitly all that he knows of Revelation.[13]

---

[11] See p.43.
[12] Rom. 3:24; *ST,* I-II, Q.113, A.2; Trent VI, Can. 11.
[13] See p.20, about how explicit that faith must be.

Note that the inner virtue of faith will incline the soul not only to believe the truth, but also to reject the errors opposed to it. Thus if someone was validly baptized as a child in a Protestant sect (at a valid baptism, God gives the true virtue of faith, *i.e.,* the Catholic Faith), when he grows up, this inner grace he received will incline him to reject the errors he hears from the Protestant minister. He may accept that minister's words when he says: "Jesus is Savior"; but he will have to reject them when he says: "Nothing is commanded in the Gospel except faith, and everything else is indifferent, neither prescribed, nor prohibited, but free," or "unbelief is the only sin that is mortal," or "grace once received can be lost by no other sin, regardless of its gravity or enormity, except unbelief" ("once saved always saved").[14] If he does not correspond to this inner grace of faith, and consciously accepts the Protestant errors in spite of that clear inner grace of faith inclining him to reject them, he loses the virtue of faith, and thus sanctifying grace. If he remains puzzled and hesitates, yet not fully accepting these errors, we should not judge him, but leave all judgment to God, "who searches the hearts" (Ps. 7:10). In all cases, we should not judge the individual since we cannot know his heart, but we must rather pray for him and exhort him and warn him of the necessity of the Catholic Faith and charity and unity!

Note that the lives of the saints show that an error on a complicated point of doctrine is not incompatible with faith: even Doctors of the Church have erred or been unclear on some points of doctrine such as the compatibility of the dogma of the Immaculate Conception and of the fact that even our Lady needed to be saved by Jesus Christ. However, these saints were rather searching for the truth than asserting in a definite way their erroneous opinion: there was no pertinacity in their error. How much more easily such error can be found among people who have been less exposed to the doctrine of the Church! Yet the inner virtue of faith in those with baptism of desire will incline them not to be pertinacious in these errors.

Pertinacity in an error against a dogma is incompatible with the virtue of faith, and thus with salvation.

---

[14] Trent, VI, Can. 19 & 27, Dz. 829, 837.

One Direct Consequence Of What Has Been Said So Far Is That These Souls Belong To The Mystical Body Of Christ, Which Is The Catholic Church

St. Thomas, in his only question in the whole *Summa* dealing with the Church (*ST*, III, Q.8), teaches that union "*in actu*–in act" with Christ is essentially by sanctifying grace with faith, hope and charity (Art. 3). Those who do not have the faith are only united with Him "*in potentia*," *i.e.*, they *can* become united with Him, but are not yet united with Him. Now baptism of desire is precisely the direct gift of this sanctifying grace, with faith, hope and charity to the soul. Hence these souls are united *in actu–in deed* with Christ and His Church, though their bond is not complete. Thus this Catholic doctrine on baptism of desire is far from opposed to the dogma "Outside of the Catholic Church there is no salvation!" The exterior union with the Church by profession of the Catholic Faith, communion in the same sacraments, and submission to the authorities of the Church, is just the direct consequence of interior faith, hope and charity. Hence charity cannot be possessed without having the *votum–desire, i.e.,* the firm will and resolution of completing the union with the Church by receiving baptism and being fully subject to Church authority. This is manifest especially in the case of the fervent catechumens, who are earnestly preparing their baptism and already follow the directives of the Church.

The doctrine of baptism of desire is useful to manifest the primacy of the interior union with Christ, by the true faith, "living faith" (see Jas. 2:26), "Faith working through charity" (Gal. 6:5). The exterior union with the Church, having baptism of water but without this living faith, is not sufficient for salvation!

How Does One Receive This Sanctifying Grace?

It may be at the time one is taking instructions to become Catholic, *e.g.*, as a catechumen. Thus in the mission countries, where the missionary was passing every six months, a catechumen who already believed and practiced the Catholic Faith, though he was not yet baptized, if he died in such a state, could go to heaven. This may be the most common case. This first example is the one given in the *Catechism of the Council of Trent*.

It may be through the ministry of angels, as all the just of the Old Testament.[15]

It may be through reading the Holy Bible. For example, suppose a Protestant missionary in Siberia dropped a Bible at someone's home. If the person reads it and, through the grace of Christ, believes and puts in practice what God says there (the Bible is Catholic!), that person has Catholic faith and charity and could go to heaven if he or she dies before being baptized.

It can simply be through the grace of an interior light, which God can grant to whomever He wants because He is Almighty![16]

God is not limited in His means! His Almighty Power is Infinite Mercy!

---

[15] See also the second example of Chartres, p.85.
[16] See the first example, p.84.

SOME LIBERAL ERRORS

Fr. Leonard Feeney reacted against the Liberals.

The insidious heresy that there may be salvation outside the Catholic Church and that submission to the Supreme Pontiff is not necessary for salvation has been taught by implication in many ways but is now getting to be more and more of an explicit teaching.

In more than one way people are made to believe that a man may be saved in any religion provided he is sincere, that a man may have baptism of desire even while explicitly refusing baptism of water, that a man may belong to the soul of the Church while persisting in his enmity to the Holy Catholic Church, indeed even while actively persecuting the Church.[17]

There was certainly need of correcting these liberal errors. Needless to say, these errors have spread everywhere with the ecumenism of Vatican II.

DOES SINCERITY WITH IGNORANCE SAVE?

The constant teaching of the Church is that sincerity with ignorance does not save. It is "faith working through charity" that counts (Gal. 5:6). Invincible ignorance of the truth of Faith excuses from a sin against faith, but it does not forgive the other sins. The principles of natural law are written in the hearts of all men (who have the use of their reason), especially: "Don't do to others what you do not want them to do to you."

For example, a native in New Caledonia two hundred years ago who never heard of Christ was not guilty of a sin against faith, but that did not excuse him from cannibalism. At the Last Judgment, he will not be able to say: "I had no chance, I never had a missionary." There is no need of a missionary to know, "Thou shalt not eat thy neighbor!"

---

[17] Catherine Goddard Clarke, *The Loyolas and the Cabots*, pp.159,160.

Closer to us, in our modern pagan world, a mother does not need a missionary to tell her: "Thou shalt not kill thy little baby in thy womb." Every fiber of her being tells her she is made to give life and love her children. Her "sincerity" and "invincible ignorance" of the truths of Faith are incapable of forgiving her sin of abortion, though she may not be guilty of a sin against faith.

To think that invincible ignorance of the truths of Faith is sufficient to excuse all sins is akin to the condemned proposition: "there is no mortal sin except infidelity" (Dz. 837).

This is what St. Paul says of *ignorance*: "This then I say and testify in the Lord: That henceforward you walk not as also the Gentiles walk in the vanity of their mind: having their understanding darkened: being alienated from the life of God through the ignorance that is in them, because of the blindness of their hearts, who despairing have given themselves up to lasciviousness, unto the working of all uncleanness, unto covetousness" (Eph 4:17-19). Is he not describing today's world?

Sins are forgiven only through the infusion of sanctifying grace,[18] which goes with the virtues of faith (Catholic!),[19] hope and charity. This infusion of grace is normally given for the first time in Baptism, which has been established by Our Lord Jesus Christ in order to give this grace to sinners: it is ***the*** means given by Our Lord to receive it for the first time. (Yet the Author of grace is not limited by the means He established.)

WHAT ABOUT THE "GOOD HEATHEN"?

It is a very common error of the modern world to believe that there is such a thing as a "good heathen." No, without the grace of Christ, no one can be good, avoiding all mortal sins! To deny this is the Pelagian heresy.

One must remember that the moral law does not only contain the last seven commandments. Please, do not forget the first three! Pagan worship and any false worship are against the First Commandment and are very grievously sinful. Thus idol worship, practices of witchcraft, Buddhism or Hinduist worship are against the moral law.

---

[18] *ST*, I-II, Q.109, A.7; Q.113, A.2.
[19] *Ibid.*, Q.113, A.4.

The subjection of the intelligence to God is an essential part of the moral law. St. Paul wants "to bring into captivity every intelligence unto the obedience of Christ" (II Cor. 10:5). Moreover, if one neglects the first three Commandments, he will be led to neglect the last seven. If one does not honor God, he will lose respect for his neighbor, created to the image and likeness of God; if he does not give "glory to God in the highest," he will not enjoy the "peace on earth to men of good will." Hence the false utopia of the meeting at Assisi.[20]

Many wrongly think that, away from the Church, one can keep the moral law without the grace of Christ. It is the constant teaching of the Church that it is not possible to keep the whole natural law without the grace of Christ! By the sole forces of our nature, it is possible to do some good, but not all our duty. Man's nature, wounded by original sin, can keep some moral commandments, but not all of them. At each given occasion, man can avoid sin (thus he is guilty if he does fall), yet without the grace of Christ he cannot persevere in all times of temptation. To say the contrary would be the heresy of Pelagius, which is very common among modern Liberals![21]

If, without the grace of Christ, one can live righteously and go to heaven, then Our Lord Jesus Christ is no longer *the* Savior!

Why would Christ have come down from heaven, if man did not need Him to be saved?

The Church also taught that it is not possible even to merit the beginning of justification. Indeed, before being justified, one is not yet just, one is a sinner, and, on his own, only merits condemnation. The Council of Orange says:

> He is an adversary of the Apostolic teaching, who says that the increase of faith as well as the beginning of faith and the very desire of faith—by which we believe in Him who justifies the unjustified, and by which we come to the regeneration of sacred baptism—inheres in us naturally and not by a gift of grace. This grace is the inspiration of the Holy Ghost, guiding our will away from infidelity to faith, from godlessness to piety. For St. Paul says: "By grace you have been saved through faith; and that not

---

[20] The scandalous ecumenical meeting arranged by Pope John Paul II was held at Assisi, Italy, October 27, 1986.
[21] See Dz. 178, 1011.

from yourselves, for it is the gift of God" (Eph. 2:8). For those who say that it is a natural faith by which we believe in God, teach that all those who are separated from the Church of Christ are, in a certain sense, believers.[22]

Note that this last sentence is the condemnation of Karl Rahner, who teaches that everyone is an implicit Christian. (A good missionary answered one day, "and many theologians are implicit pagans!") Note also the insistence of the Council on *grace*, rather than on the *character* of baptism.

And the grace of Christ cannot be had without the Faith, true Faith, of course, which is the Catholic Faith.

Is Baptism of Desire Very Common?

It is a common opinion among Liberals that there are "millions upon millions" (Fr. Most's article, *The Wanderer*, February 5, 1987) who receive this baptism of desire.

Did these Liberals go into mission lands? If you talk with missionaries, you will be astonished to see how much the people to whom they went to preach Christ really needed Him. Pagan Rome was the "Mistress of all errors" (St. Leo the Great). Some Indians in Latin America, before the arrival of the missionaries, had human sacrifices. In New Caledonia, they were eating each other; in Africa they were hating each other (tribal hatred and families' hatred were passed from generation to generation!); when the civilized governments left some of these countries by an irrational "decolonization" it happened that one tribe systematically wiped out another (*e.g.,* in Biafra). In all these countries, before the arrival of the missionaries, sorcerers were ruling, *i.e.,* the Devil through these sorcerers. And our Western countries were no better: remember the abominable corruption of the Greeks and Romans before the arrival of the Apostles, described by St. Paul (Rom. 1:22-32).

And in our modern world, departing more and more from God, from Christ, one can see the increase of violence, impurities, drugs, injustices, thefts, culminating in abortion, euthanasia, *etc*.

Many missionaries, including the American martyrs, were martyred by those to whom they preached. Our Liberals do not

---

[22] Dz. 178.

want to be martyrs, so they imagine that these poor souls, who do not know Christ, do not need to know Him: these Liberals will be asked to account for not having preached the truths of Faith to them. "If, when I say to the wicked, thou shalt surely die; thou declare it not to him, nor speak to him, that he may be converted from his wicked way and live: the same wicked man shall die in his iniquity, but I will require his blood at thy hand" (Ez. 3:18).

Our Lord Jesus Christ did not say to His Apostles: "Sit here, I will give baptism of desire to all nations!" He rather said: "Go, teach all nations, baptizing them in the name of the Father and of the Son and of the Holy Ghost, teaching them to observe all things whatsoever I have commanded you" (Mt. 28:19, 20).

Now if someone has received sanctifying grace before baptism, which, as shown above, is possible and does happen (though it is like a miracle of grace), one must add that it is quite difficult to keep that grace without the help of the sacraments (*e.g.,* if he is in Siberia, or in a pagan country). It already requires great efforts to keep that grace and persevere until the end for those who are in the Church;[23] how much more difficult it is for those who do not have all these benefits! It is not difficult to be saved if we take seriously the gifts of Our Lord Jesus Christ (His teaching and sacraments) and put them in practice (Mt. 7:24-27), but if one does not have at his disposal the means established by Christ to give us His grace, and lives in a pagan or heretical surrounding against which he must constantly fight, it is quite difficult!

The Liberals, who would have us think that it is easy to be saved without the help of the sacraments instituted by Christ precisely to apply to us the grace of His salvation, practically make this holy institution useless! Why would Christ have instituted them if it is so easy to be saved without them?

We must rather hold that because of the extreme difficulty to be saved without them, Christ has instituted these sacraments precisely to help us!

Salvation by baptism of desire alone is like a miracle; God does perform miracles, but one must add that miracles are rare, both in the natural order and in the supernatural order. Baptism

---

[23] "The kingdom of God suffereth violence, and the violent bear it away" (Mt. 11:12).

of desire being like a miracle of the supernatural order, it would be presumptuous to affirm that there are relatively many such souls saved by baptism of desire only. There are certainly such souls in heaven,[24] but they remain the exceptions to the rule, the rule being the Law of Baptism as set by Our Lord Jesus Christ. Yet such exceptions do exist; and one could add that there are probably more numerous miracles in the supernatural order than in the natural order, because they are more directly connected with the salvation of souls, which is the purpose of all that Divine Providence does for mankind.

Note here that some of Fr. Feeney's followers say that the salvation of any man is a miracle. St. Thomas does not agree: salvation does not exceed the power of its proper cause, which is God.[25] To be saved by the grace of God, using faithfully the means put at our disposal by Our Lord Jesus Christ, belongs to the ordinary Providence of God, "who wants all men to be saved" (I Tim. 2:4). But when God Himself bypasses His laws and gives sanctifying grace to a soul without the normal means He had established, this is like a miracle and therefore is rare.

FAITH ENTIRELY IMPLICIT?

An explicit knowledge of all the articles of Faith has never been absolutely required! It is necessary not to deny any one of them knowingly; but it is not necessary to know all of them explicitly. By believing the Catholic Church, we believe virtually all the deposit of Faith entrusted to her. It is sufficient to believe all that one knows of Divine Revelation. But it is necessary to know and believe something divinely revealed.

The popes (Pope Clement XI, Dz. 1349ab) and Doctors (*ST,* II-II, Q.2, A.7-8) have taught that it is necessary to know explicitly the essential articles of Faith, the Trinity, the Incarnation and Redemption, in as much as they have been revealed to the person,

---

[24] St. Alphonsus: "It is *de fide [it belongs to the Faith]* that there are souls saved by baptism of desire" (see p.77).

[25] *ST,* I-II, Q.114, A.10. This is the reason why I wrote that baptism of desire is *like* a miracle: its proper cause is God, and as such it does not exceed the power of its proper cause; but it bypasses the ordinary means set by God to produce the effect of the supernatural birth, and as such it is *like* a miracle.

i.e., not necessarily with all the theological wording, but with the exactitude of the Catholic Faith.[26]

Our Lord Himself said: "I am the good shepherd, and I know mine and *mine know Me*" (Jn. 10:14).

St. Paul says that God "wants all men to be saved and to come to the knowledge of the truth" (I Tim. 2:4).

> For there is not distinction of the Jew and the Greek: for the same is Lord over all, rich unto all that call upon him. *For whosoever shall call upon the name of the Lord, shall be saved.* How then shall they call on him, in Whom they have not believed? Or *how shall they believe Him, of whom they have not heard?* And how shall they hear, without a preacher? And how shall they preach unless they be sent, as it is written: How beautiful are the feet of them that preach the gospel of peace, of them that bring glad tidings of good things! But all do not obey the Gospel. For Isaias saith: Lord, who hath believed our report? *Faith then cometh by hearing; and hearing by the word of Christ.* But I say: Have they not heard? Yes, verily, their sound hath gone forth into all the earth, and their words unto the ends of the whole world (Rom. 10:12-18).

St. Thomas teaches:

> It is written "There is no other name under heaven given to men, whereby we must be saved" (Acts 4:12). Therefore belief of some kind in the mystery of Christ's Incarnation was necessary at all times and for all persons, but this belief differed according to differences of times and persons....After grace had been revealed, both learned and simple folk are bound to explicit faith in the mysteries of Christ.[27]

However, how much is exactly necessary to know explicitly is a question which has not been settled.

In any case, it is important to point out that without a supernatural object, there could not be the supernatural virtue of faith, much less a supernatural act of faith; and a supernatural object can only be known through revelation (through a missionary, through the Bible, through an angel, through an inner light). Pope Pius IX says: "through the work of the divine light and grace."[28] The gift of grace by which we are saved includes the revelation of some supernatural truth, at least the essential mysteries.

---

[26] See the example of Job, p.23.

In the *Summa Theologica*, (I-II, Q.113, A.3-5), St. Thomas explains that in the process of justification of an adult, having the use of his reason, there is need of a movement of the free will, including a movement of faith and a movement of perfect contrition: no one can be justified if he would remain in complete (even invincible!) ignorance of the Faith! When the Church speaks of a possible "implicit desire," what is implicit is the doctrine of the sacraments, not the whole doctrine of Christ. St. Augustine had said before: "He Who created you without you, shall not justify you without you."[29] Note that an infant, not having yet the use of his reason, has no other possibility to be saved than through the actual reception of the sacrament of baptism, *i.e.*, baptism of water.

The Council of Trent gives great authority to that teaching of St. Thomas:

> [Adults] are disposed for justification in this way: awakened and assisted by divine grace, they conceive faith "from hearing" (Rom. 10:7), and they are freely led to God, believing that the divine Revelation and promises are true, especially that the unjustified man is justified by God's grace "through the redemption which is in Christ Jesus" (Rom. 3:24); next they know that they are sinners; and by turning from a salutary fear of divine justice to a consideration of God's mercy, they are encouraged to hope, confident that God will be propitious to them for Christ's sake. They begin to love God as the source of all justice and are thereby moved by a sort of hatred and detestation for sin,

---

[27] *ST*, II-II, Q.2, A.7. In this article, St. Thomas teaches that, in the Old Testament, the common of the people could have a mere implicit faith in Christ, "under the veil of the sacrifices" required in the Old Law, believing what their leaders and Prophets knew explicitly; he also teaches (ad 3) that among the Gentiles "if, however, some were saved without receiving any revelation, [the objection to which he answers referring to the "ministry of Angels," he means 'public revelation' like that to the Hebrews; he does not mean 'without absolutely any revelation'] they were not saved without faith in the Mediator, for though they did not believe in Him explicitly, they did nevertheless, have implicit Faith through believing in Divine Providence, since they believed that God would deliver mankind in whatever way was pleasing to Him, and *according to the revelation of the Spirit to those who knew the truth.*" This last phrase refers to private revelations, made to Gentiles like Job, "who knew the truth." St. Augustine gives other examples.

[28] Dz. 1677; see also the first example, p.84.

[29] Sermon 169, p.661, *Biblioteca de los Autores Católicos* (henceforth BAC).

that is, by the penance that must be done before baptism. Finally, they determine to receive baptism, begin a new life, and keep the Divine Commandments.[30]

Though it is evident that explicit knowledge of the quotes of St. Paul is not required, the doctrine remains that an act of faith in what one knows of Revelation ("through hearing" either externally or at least internally as in the case of Job), an act of hope, an act of charity and an act of contrition are required.

By the very nature of faith, it is impossible that it be completely implicit! Faith is a light to the intelligence. Though not as perfect as the Beatific Vision, the light of faith is incompatible with complete ignorance of the supernatural truths. It is false to say that the knowledge of supernatural truths can be attained just through our natural reasoning, thus faith in the natural providence of God is not sufficient alone. Implicit faith in some points of doctrine is not included in ignorance, but only in explicit faith in other articles of doctrine! Therefore there is need of explicit faith in some article of Faith.

Since the whole supernatural order is centered and summed up in Our Lord Jesus Christ, explicit faith in Jesus Christ is necessary for salvation. The act of faith needs to be faith in Jesus Christ in a precise and unambiguous way, though it does not need to have the explicit theological wording. For example, if a pagan witnessed the holy death of a martyr such as St. Martina, with the accompanying miracles, and, touched by the grace of God, would stand up and profess his faith in Jesus Christ, saying: "I believe in the God of Martina!" he knew explicitly that Jesus Christ, professed by Martina, was the true God, but he knew very little else of Jesus Christ, much less about the Sacraments. His act of faith had the precision of the Catholic Faith of the martyr, to which it conformed itself, but contained only implicitly the whole Catholic doctrine!

It is worth noting that a missionary is not always necessary. In the Old Testament, the holy man Job did not belong to the chosen people, and may not have heard of the revelation received by Abraham and his descendants (nowhere does he refer to it). Yet he had an unambiguous faith in Jesus Christ; he made a beautiful

---

[30] Dz. 798.

profession of Faith: "For I know that my Redeemer is living, and in the last day I shall rise out of the earth, and I shall be clothed again with my skin, and in my flesh I shall see my God, Whom I myself shall see, and my eyes shall behold, and not another: this my hope is laid up in my bosom" (Job 19:25-27). To see God with the eyes of his flesh would be impossible without the Incarnation; thus by these words Job professes his faith in God Incarnate, Jesus Christ.

How was he instructed? In his sleep: "By a dream, in a vision by night, when deep sleep falleth upon men, and they are sleeping in their beds: then He openeth the ears of men, and teaching instructeth them in what they are to learn" (Job 33:15, 16). What God did in the Old Testament, He can do in the New Testament too! However, one must remember that in the Old Testament, God was using angels in a normal way, while after the Incarnation took place, He uses men, *i.e.*, missionaries, in a normal way: such illuminations in a vision are certainly still possible[31] though they are no longer the normal way of God to instruct souls. In His goodness, God wants to associate men with this wonderful work of redemption of souls, by making them His missionaries!

In any case, there is no baptism of desire without the supernatural virtue of faith–the True Faith!–and a certain explicit knowledge of the essential points of Faith.

"I Was Hungry..."

> I was interested in the missions not only from a practical point of view of helping, but also from a theological point of view. I studied and read so many things about what we used to call "the salvation of pagans," how are these unbelievers saved? In the 11th century,[32] we were given the theology of baptism of desire.
>
> But when you travel the world, visit leper colonies, see human beings fighting with vultures in the garbage heaps of Latin America, when you see the poverty of the great cities of the world, when you see 250,000 sleeping in the streets of Calcutta

---

[31] See p.105.
[32] St. Bernard, to whom Bishop Sheen probably refers here, is far from the first to have taught this doctrine; St. Bernard himself refers to St. Augustine and St. Ambrose (4th century), and one finds it even earlier in St. Cyprian (3rd century).

every night, when you see starving women with starving children strapped on their backs in India; when I saw all these things, I never saw so many Christs in my life, I saw them everywhere, maybe I saw more there than here, but in a different way.

When you say that they do not know Christ, *they don't need to know!* (emphasis in original). "I was hungry, I was naked, I was homeless..." When? When? When? Did they know it? No! But they were carrying the burden of Christ, and this is their salvation.[33]

As much as I revere and esteem Bishop Fulton Sheen for many truly excellent conferences, especially on the sacrifice of Our Lord Jesus Christ, it is impossible for me to agree to the thesis he expressed in this particular passage.

Indeed, the more one suffers, the more one needs Our Lord Jesus Christ: he does need to know Him, to believe in Him, to hope in Him, to love Him. When everything on earth is failing him, Jesus alone is able to give him hope!

What did Our Lord Jesus Christ Himself say about those who suffer? "Come to me all you who labor, and are burdened, and I will refresh you. Take up my yoke upon you, and learn of me, because I am meek, and humble of heart: and you shall find rest for your souls. For my yoke is sweet and my burden light" (Mt. 11:28-30). How could they come to Him if they do not know Him? How then can one say, "They don't need to know Him?" More than anyone else, they do need to know, believe and love Jesus Christ, our Savior. And we have the duty, not only to give them medicine for the body, but above all to give them this Divine Remedy, this Divine Physician of their soul as much as of their body. The goal of missionaries is first of all to heal the souls, and only as a preparation and as a consequence do they heal the bodies.

That we have to see Christ in those who suffer does not mean that they themselves do not need Christ! In a similar way, we ought to see Christ in the authorities, civil and religious; but that does not mean that they themselves do not need Christ!

---

[33] Bishop Fulton Sheen, *Suffering–The Passion of Christ Continued*, (Ramsey, NJ: Keep the Faith) cassette tape.

THE ROOTS OF THE LIBERAL ERRORS

The root of all these liberal errors is two fold: in the intelligence, the denial of, or at least the tendency to reduce the objectivity of truth, and in the will, a sterile pity.

They over-emphasize the subjective conditions of the person (good faith, ignorance, sincerity, the Rights of Man...); they think that any faith is good and saves.

But truth is objective, *i.e.*, independent of the conditions of the subject. No matter what we Catholics think, no matter what pagans, Muslims, Jews, or Protestants think, in the One God there are Three Divine Persons, the Father, the Son and the Holy Ghost: this mystery of the Holy Trinity, though spiritual, is an objective truth, it is the truth! We Catholics did not *make* it, we *learned* it from Christ, *i.e.*, from the Incarnate Word of God Himself!

For example, if there is poison hidden in a cake, no amount of ignorance or sincerity will protect the person who eats it! Similarly, the poison of error hidden in any false religion is going to hurt the souls who adhere to these false religions, no matter how sincere or ignorant they may be!

If this ignorance is the result of negligence to search for and learn the truth, it does not totally excuse from unbelief, but merely diminishes the culpability, according to St. Paul:

> ...all seduction of iniquity to them that perish; because they receive not the love of the truth, that they might be saved. Therefore God shall send them the operation of error, to believe lying: that all may be judged who have not believed the truth, but have consented to iniquity (II Thess. 2:10-12).

If a soul, placed in the environment of a false religion, corresponds to the actual graces that God gives to it, then these lights will help the soul to see the objective truth, thus detaching that soul from the errors in that false religion, causing it to no longer adhere to it.

You will notice that this root of the liberal errors is the opposite of the root of Fr. Feeney's error (see p.110). The Liberals put too much emphasis on the interior dispositions of soul, losing from sight or even denying the objectivity of truth; Fr. Feeney puts too much emphasis on the exterior reception of the sacrament of baptism rather than on the interior grace of baptism. The proper Catholic position is summed up in these words of our Lord Jesus Christ: "The true adorers shall adore the Father in spirit and in truth. For the Father also seeketh such to adore Him. God is a spirit; and they that adore Him, must adore Him in spirit and in truth" (Jn. 4:23, 24). "In spirit": primacy of the spiritual over the external; "and in truth": primacy of the objective truth over the subjective dispositions.

The second root is a sterile pity: the Liberals pity "the poor souls who have no chance," but they do nothing to help these souls to be saved! What would you think of a doctor who would, out of a sterile pity for his dying patients, console them and tell them that, if they are sincere and think everything will be alright, they are in good health and need not worry? The good doctor, on the contrary, would do something and provide the proper remedy. The remedy for all souls is Our Lord and Savior Jesus Christ! "Neither is there salvation in any other. For there is no other name under heaven given to men whereby we must be saved" (Acts 4:12). True pity and mercy for the unbelievers should push all of us to "go, and teach all nations" (Mt. 28:19), giving them Jesus Christ!

IF GOD IS SO GOOD, HOW CAN HE LET ALL THESE PAGANS BE DAMNED?

The first truth to state is that God gives sufficient graces to all men to be saved. Indeed God "wants all men to be saved and to come to the knowledge of the truth." And "God does not command the impossible, but, with His command, He exhorts you to do what you can, to pray for what you cannot, and He helps so that you can."[34] Thus on the one hand we know the goodness of God, the greatest proof of it being that "God so loved the world, as to give His only begotten Son, that whosoever believeth in Him may not perish, but may have life everlasting" (Jn. 3:16). He gave Him not only at the Incarnation, but He delivered Him to be crucified for our salvation! Our Lord Jesus Christ wants our salva-

---

[34] St. Augustine, *De Natura et Gratia*, C. 43, No. 50 (see Council of Trent, Sess. 6, Chap. 11, Dz. 804).

tion, and that of our neighbor, more than we want it ourselves: He died on the Cross for it!

On the other hand, we know His perfect justice. All those who are good go to heaven, all those who are wicked go to hell; only the good go to heaven, only the wicked go to hell. And the good are good by the grace of Christ, the wicked are wicked by their own wickedness.[35]

Modern man rejects guilt; he does not want to acknowledge his own guilt, and has a bad tendency to excuse the criminal and incriminate the victim. But his excuses will have no value at the Last Judgment!

As to know how many are saved, and how many are not saved, and why so many souls are lost, is the mystery of the Divine choice of His elect, which we must adore and not discuss!

> O man, who art thou that replieth against God? Shall the thing formed say to him that formed it: Why hast thou made me thus? Or hath not the potter power over the clay, of the same lump, to make one vessel unto honor, and another unto dishonor? What if God, willing to shew his wrath, and to make his power known, endured with much patience vessels of wrath, fitted for destruction, that he might shew the riches of his glory on the vessels of mercy, which he hath prepared unto glory?... (Rom. 9:20-23).
>
> O the depth of the riches of the wisdom and of the knowledge of God! How incomprehensible are His judgments, and how unsearchable His ways! For who hath known the mind of the Lord? Or who hath been His counselor? Or who hath first given to Him, and recompense shall be made Him? For of Him, and by Him, and in Him, are all things: to Him be glory for ever. Amen (Rom. 11:33-36).

To the question, "Lord, are they few that are saved?" Our Lord answered: "Strive to enter by the narrow gate!" (Lk. 13:24). To this speculative question, Our Lord gave a practical answer, as St. Paul: "Know you not that they that run in a race, all run in-

---

[35] God is the first cause of all good; man must cooperate in good works, he is a second cause of them, in dependence on God. But God is not the first cause of evil: it is the free creature that is responsible for sin and evil. Since good is above evil, it is easy to understand that the first cause of good is above the first cause of evil.

deed, but one receiveth the prize? So run that you may obtain!" (I Cor. 9:24).

With Pope Pius XII, one can give to the above question the following practical answer.

God does not want all these pagans to be damned, He wants you to pray for them, He wants you to make sacrifices for them, He wants you to "sanctify yourself for them" (Jn. 17:19); He wants you "to go and teach all nations, baptizing them in the name of the Father and of the Son and of the Holy Ghost!" (Mt. 20:19).

Remember the words of our Lady to St. Catherine Labouré. St. Catherine saw beams of light from the jewels on the hands of our Lady going down towards the earth, and she noticed jewels without such beams. Wondering about this, she asked our Lady, who answered: "These are the graces men fail to ask of me!" Also our Lady taught the children of Fatima: "Many souls go to hell because there is no one to pray and make sacrifices for them!"

The treasure of Faith has not been given to you so that you hide it in the earth like the useless servant (Mt. 25:25); you must make it fructify, you must give it to others! It is a wonderful Providence of God to call you to be His instrument in the work of salvation of souls; if you fail to heed His call, then souls will be lost because of you. Remember the words of God to Ezechiel:

> If, when I say to the wicked, Thou shalt surely die: thou declare it not to him, nor speak to him, that he may be converted from his wicked way and live: the same wicked man shall die in his iniquity, but I will require his blood at thy hand (Ez. 3:18).

Therefore those who make no effort to work for the conversion of their neighbor to the true Faith of Christ, hiding their spiritual torpor under a false notion of "salvation by invincible ignorance," have no right to criticize God in His providence; they have only to blame their lack of zeal if they think there are "too many" souls lost!

Those who pray, sacrifice themselves and work for the conversion of souls will have the joy of seeing many souls returning to Our Lord Jesus Christ; but they will also understand more easily by their own experience that "the perverse are hard to be corrected, and the number of fools is infinite" (Eccles. 1:15). They also understand these words of Our Lord Jesus Christ: "Enter ye in at the narrow gate: for wide is the gate, and broad is the way that leadeth to destruction, and many there are who go in there at. How narrow is the gate, and strait is the way that leadeth to life: and few there are that find it!" (Mt. 7:13,14).

Our Lord does everything to awaken the slothfulness of souls; but some choose to deceive themselves under the pretext of the "goodness of God, who is not going to damn so many souls," rather than to take seriously the words of our Divine Savior. O you, who cover up your sloth under the name of the goodness of God, since God is so good, get up from your sleep (Rom. 13:11), love Him with your whole heart, and share His truth and love with as many souls as possible!

You might say, "Your solution is wrong because how can I, alone, convert so many souls?" I answer that indeed, you alone cannot; but just think if every Catholic would take seriously his Faith, put it in practice with fervor, and be missionary around him, all the world would be converted in a short time! The reason why there are still so many who do not know Christ properly is because of the culpable apathy and lukewarmness of Catholics!

This solution is that of Pope Pius XII, relying on St. Augustine, in his encyclical on the Church: "And if many, alas! still err far from the Catholic Truth and do not want to follow the inspirations of the divine grace, the reason is that, not only their own selves, but the Christian faithful themselves do not address more fervent prayers to God for this end!"[36]

Note also that those who do pray and make sacrifices for the salvation of their neighbor, believing that "outside the Catholic Church, there is no salvation," can obtain from the Divine Mercy a miracle of grace, such as baptism of desire.[37]

---

[36] *Mystici Corporis*, No.839.
[37] See the beautiful story of Fr. Augustine of the Blessed Sacrament on p.84.

THE TEACHING OF THE CHURCH ON BAPTISM OF BLOOD AND BAPTISM OF DESIRE

Overview

Reading the history of Fr. Feeney's and the St. Benedict Center's fight against the Liberals in and out of Boston, it seems that what they really oppose are the errors of the Liberals, and that an exposition of the Church's teaching on Baptism of Blood and Baptism of Desire that remains faithful to the dogma *outside the Church there is no salvation*, would be accepted by them. In fact, the first edition of this book has helped some of them, and I wish and pray that this second edition will help more. I am convinced that an honest Catholic, bringing to this study an attitude of faith, that is, of humble submission to the teaching of the Church, cannot do otherwise than embrace the doctrine so unanimously taught by the popes, the Fathers, the Doctors and the saints on baptism of blood and baptism of desire. He will find in this book abundant quotations of theirs to see clearly what is their teaching.

However, after that first edition, which was then a small booklet of sixty-two pages, whole books have been written pretending to refute it.[38] They present two kinds of arguments as refutation, arguments of authority, which we will see in this section, and some arguments from reason, which we will answer in the next section. In fact, for the honest reader, the first edition was already sufficient refutation of such writings. Having been out of print for more than a year, a second edition was necessary. Having

---

[38] *Can Only Baptized Roman Catholics Enter the Kingdom of Heaven–Father Feeney and the Truth About Salvation*, by Bro. Robert Mary, MICM Tert., St. Benedict Center, Richmond (235pp.); see also *Who Shall Ascend?* by Fr. James Wathen, (689 pages! pp.81-100); *Desire and Deception,* by Thomas A. Hutchinson.

put much additional material here, it has been reordered for greater clarity.

Allow me here a short overview, in order to keep the important points in mind. The core error of the followers of Fr. Feeney is that they hold their own *private interpretation* of some passages of the Scripture, rejecting the interpretation given by the Councils, Fathers and Doctors of these same passages; they also hold their own private interpretation of some other quotes of the Councils and Doctors, *as if* these quotes were against the explicit and unanimous teaching of the Catholic Church. Their private interpretation is that the necessity of belonging to the Church requires absolutely the necessity of receiving *in re* the baptism of water, and that the necessity of baptism of water is so absolute a necessity, that it excludes baptism of blood and baptism of desire. Their thesis is so exclusive that any Doctor or saint supporting baptism of blood is a testimony against their position.

They completely forget that the holy Doctors that they reject *have been approved by the Church on the very points that they reject*: the passages of St. Ambrose and St. Augustine are cited by almost every single Doctor and theologian who treat this subject, and have even been explicitly referred to by a pope. They are absolutely unable to bring a single ecclesiastical author, much less a saint, a Doctor or a pope, who explicitly says that St. Cyprian, St. Ambrose, St. Augustine, St. Thomas, *etc.*, were *wrong on the particular point of baptism of blood and of desire*. So much for the arguments of authority that they bring.

What is the authority of that teaching on baptism of blood and baptism of desire? That of the *ordinary and universal magisterium of the Church*. It is clearly the doctrine universally taught in every Catholic university since the beginning of Scholasticism (Peter Lombard). The catechisms in most dioceses, following the *Catechism of the Council of Trent* and of St. Pius X, teach it explicitly. Moreover, the Canon Law published by Benedict XV gives indubitably great confirmation of this.

The Authority of the Scriptures

JOHN 3:5

Fr. Feeney's greatest argument was that Our Lord's words, "Unless a man be born again of water and the Holy Ghost, he cannot enter into the kingdom of God" (Jn. 3:5) mean the absolute necessity of baptism of water *in re* with no exception whatsoever. This neglects the very first principle of interpretation of the Holy Scripture, solemnly given by the Council of Trent and repeated at Vatican I: "That sense of Sacred Scripture is to be considered as true which holy Mother Church has held and now holds; for it is her office to judge about the true sense and interpretation of Sacred Scripture; and therefore, no one is allowed to interpret Sacred Scripture contrary to this sense nor contrary to the unanimous agreement of the Fathers" (Dz. 1788, see Dz. 786).

The great question is, then, how did the Church explain these words of Our Lord? How did the popes, the Fathers, the Doctors, the saints explain them?

Since the argument of authority has more importance in matters of Faith than anyone's personal analysis of the text,[39] I put here first the most authoritative explanation, that of the Council of Trent. This dogmatic Council quotes twice this verse, once explaining the word "water" as being "true and natural water" (Dz. 858), and the other time explaining the word "unless..." as expressing a necessity *"re aut voto*–in fact or in desire": "After the promulgation of the Gospel this passing (from sin to justice) *cannot take place without the water of regeneration or the desire for it, as it is written*: 'unless a man be born again of water and the Holy Ghost, he cannot enter into the kingdom of God'" (Dz. 796, see Dz. 847).

Any one interpreting the necessity of baptism taught by Our Lord in these words, as being other than a necessity *"re aut voto*–in fact or in desire" departs from the interpretation taught by the Council of Trent.

---

[39] *ST*, I, Q.1, A.8, ad 2.

To confirm that such is the meaning of the Council of Trent, let us read Cornelius a Lapide, the great exegete shortly after the Council of Trent, precisely in his commentary of John 3:5:

> *Reborn of water,* must be here understood either in fact or in desire [*vel reipsa vel voto*]. He who is contrite over his sins, wants baptism, and cannot receive it because of lack of water or minister, is reborn through the resolution and desire of baptism. The Council of Trent explains this verse expressly so in Session 7, Canon 4 about the sacraments in general. [40]

The Fathers have relied on these words of Our Lord to prove the necessity of the sacrament of baptism; but often without precisely saying *what kind of necessity or within what limits.* One ought not to interpret the Fathers in a manner opposed to the Council of Trent. Yet, we do find these precisions explicitly in some of the Fathers. St. Augustine explains how baptism of blood is not against these words, and supports his teaching with the Holy Scripture itself. It is essential to point out that the Fathers explicitly state "even without the water," "before they were baptized," "without baptism…" He says in the *City of God:*

> All those who, even without having received the laver of regeneration (Tit. 3:5), died for the profession of Faith in Christ, [this martyrdom] does for them as much to remit their sins, as if they were washed in the baptismal font. Indeed the same One Who said: "Unless a man be born again of water and the Holy Ghost, he cannot enter into the Kingdom of God" (Jn. 3:5), the Same said in another sentence **with no less generality**: "Every one therefore that shall confess Me before men I will also confess him before My Father who is in heaven" (Mt. 10:32). [41]

St. Thomas Aquinas explains this verse of the Gospel according to St. John: [42]

> As it is written (I Kg. 16:7), "Man seeth those things that appear, but the Lord beholdeth the heart." Now a man who desires to be "born again of water and the Holy Ghost" by baptism,

---

[40] Cornelius a Lapide, *Commentaria in Sacram Scripturam* (Naples 1857), Vol.8, p.703. In fact, the Council explains this passage in Sess. 6, Chap. 4, which is further strengthened by the anathema of Can. 4 of Sess. 7, as he says here.
[41] *De Civitate Dei,* 13:7; R.J., No.1759.
[42] *ST,* II, Q.68, A.2, ad 1.

is regenerated in the heart, though not in body; thus the Apostle says (Rom. 2:29) that "The circumcision is that of the heart, in the spirit, not in the letter; whose praise is not of men but of God."

These Fathers and Doctors, far from being reproved by the Church for their interpretation, have been followed unanimously by the Church, as will be shown later. So, applying the principle of Vatican I, it is clear that we ought to hold this same interpretation.

Explanation: The Church's interpretation of these words (Jn. 3:5) is that the *grace* of baptism (*res sacramenti*) is absolutely necessary, with no exceptions whatsoever, while the exterior water (*sacramentum tantum*) is necessary "*re aut voto*–in fact or at least in desire."[43]

First the grammatical analysis of the sentence itself shows that the word "unless" falls *directly and principally* upon "reborn" and *obliquely and secondarily* upon "by water and the Holy Ghost." In other words: *what* is necessary? Rebirth. *How* is one reborn? By water and the Holy Ghost. The immediate context itself proves this: Our Lord had just said that rebirth was necessary ("Amen, amen, I say to thee, unless a man be born again, he cannot see the kingdom of God." v.3). Nicodemus asked him: "how?" taking the word "born" in a very material way. Our Lord answers, insisting again on the necessity of the rebirth, and showing the means He established for this rebirth, *viz*., the sacrament of baptism.

Now let us consider the whole context. Within six verses, Our Lord speaks of a new birth five times (v.3, 5, 6, 7, 8), but of water only once (v.5). Explaining what He had just said in the verse in question, twice Our Lord says: "he who is born of the Spirit," (v.6, 8) without mentioning the water any more. Then in the rest of His discourse to Nicodemus, He explains how this new birth is by "living faith."

Therefore, the emphasis of the whole passage is on the spiritual rebirth, which is the grace signified and produced by the sacrament. It is thus perfectly legitimate to interpret with the Fathers that the absolute necessity applies to this spiritual rebirth, Our

---

[43] Council of Trent, Dz. 796, 847.

Lord mentioning the water as the obligatory means (necessary "*re aut voto*–in fact or in desire") to obtain that spiritual rebirth. Contrary to what the followers of Fr. Feeney pretend, the emphasis of this whole passage is not on water, but on rebirth. By holding with the Church that the rebirth is what is absolutely necessary, and that water is necessary "*re aut voto,*" one respects the truth of the words of Our Lord and the truth of the interpretation of the Church. By pretending that water itself is absolutely necessary without any exception whatsoever, one departs from the interpretation of the Church, thereby being unfaithful to Our Lord Himself.

Is John 3:5 a Law?

Bro. Robert Mary objects thus: "It is not totally correct to say that the above quote from Our Lord is a *law.* A law, strictly speaking, is a command or a prohibition. The words of Our Lord [...] are given by St. John in the form of a *proposition,* a statement of fact. It is either true or it is false. [...] God is not bound by the laws He has set. However, God *is* bound by the *propositions* He has made. [...] If God is not bound by water in terms of salvation, then we may ask, why bind Him to His word in any of His teachings?" (*op. cit.*, p.99).

His reasoning falsely presupposes that baptism of blood and baptism of desire would make Our Lord's *proposition* false. This objection had been answered many times by the best theologians (*e.g.,* St. Thomas quoted above) unanimously. For instance Billuart[44]: "He who said generally, unless one is reborn, *etc.*, has said with no less generality: everyone who believes in him shall not be confounded,[45] whosoever shall invoke the name of the Lord shall be saved,[46] he who loves Me shall be loved by My Father,[47] and other similar statements. Hence **the Church rightly understands** this general sentence of Christ *unless one is reborn* of baptism of water *in re vel in voto–in fact or in desire.*" Thus the proposition of

---

[44] *Summa Sancti Thomae,* III, p.233 (Part VI, Ch.1, A.6; he has 12 pages on baptism of desire).
[45] Rom. 9:33, 10:11, quoting Is. 28:16.
[46] St. Peter in Acts 2:21, St. Paul Rom. 10:13, both quoting Joel 2:32.
[47] Jn. 14:21; for other texts, see for instance Jn. 11:26.

Our Lord, *understood in the sense of Catholic Tradition,* remains true with baptism of blood and baptism of desire!

Moreover, Our Lord's words are not a simple proposition, but a conditional proposition, establishing the required means to obtain a desired end. Such propositions are apt to signify laws; there are many such examples in the Holy Scriptures, *e.g.*, "And the king being angry called for his priests [of the idol Bel], and said to them: If you tell me not, who it is that eateth up these expenses, you shall die."[48] There was no clearer way to *command* them to tell it.

Lastly, St. Augustine himself calls John 3:5 a law, "*lex Christi.*"[49]

A Scriptural Lesson on St. John by St. Thomas Aquinas

A parallel between the necessity of baptism (Jn. 3:5) and the necessity of the Holy Eucharist (Jn. 6:54) puts even more in light the truth of baptism of blood and baptism of desire. These two affirmations of Our Lord are very similar: "Unless a man be born again of water and the Holy Ghost, he cannot enter into the kingdom of God" (Jn. 3:5). "Amen, amen I say unto you: except you eat the flesh of the Son of man and drink His Blood, you shall not have life in you" (Jn. 6:54).

If Fr. Feeney would have applied his method of interpretation to this passage, he would have had to conclude that no one who had not received *de facto* the Holy Eucharist would have eternal life, thus baptized children who would not have received the Blessed Sacrament would not go to heaven! He did not hold this opinion, though he says these rather disconcerting words:

> I think that baptism makes you the son of God. *I do not think it makes you the child of Mary.* I think the Holy Eucharist makes you a child of Mary. What happens to those children who die between baptism and the Holy Eucharist?...They go to the Beatific Vision. They are of the Kingdom of Mary, but *they are not the children of Mary.* Mary is their Queen, but *not their Mother.* They are like little angels. There was a strong tradition in the Church that always spoke of them as "those angels who

---

[48] Dan. 14:7; see also Gen. 43:3, 44:23, Lev. 5:1, Deut. 28:58, 59, I Kg. 18:25, 19:11, Dan. 2:5.

[49] *Contra Iulianum, opus imp.* II, 161 (BAC, p.369).

died in infancy." They have the Beatific Vision, and they see the great Queen, but *not move in as part of the Mystical Body of Christ*...I say: If a child dies after having received baptism, he dies as the son of God, but *not yet as the child of Mary*...[50]

The emphasized words are at least offensive to the pious ear. Do they mean that one could go to heaven without being "part of the Mystical Body of Christ"? The Church rather taught that by baptism one was incorporated into the Mystical Body of Christ, and thus became not only a son of God, but also a child of Mary. Our Lady gave birth not only to the Head (Christ) but also to the members of His Mystical Body: there is not a single member of His Body whose Mother she is not.

Fr. Feeney should have applied to baptism the explanation beautifully exposed by St. Thomas. The reader will notice that St. Thomas refers to baptism of desire. In this passage, St. Thomas makes clear that the reality contained in the sacrament (*res sacramenti*) is absolutely necessary, in both cases of baptism and Eucharist; yet before the reception of the exterior sign (*sacramentum tantum*), the reality of the sacrament can be had by the desire of it.

Whether the Eucharist is necessary for salvation?
(*Summa Theologica*, III, Q.73, A.3)

> In this sacrament, two things have to be considered, namely, the sacrament itself and the reality contained in it.[51] Now it was stated above that the reality of the sacrament is the unity of the Mystical Body, without which there can be no salvation; for there is no entering into salvation outside the Church, just as in the time of the deluge there was none outside the Ark, which signified the Church, according to I Pet. 3:20, 21. And it has been said above (*ST*, Q.68, A.2, see p.73), that before receiving a sacrament, the reality of the sacrament can be had through the very desire[52] of receiving the sacrament. Accordingly, before the

---

[50] Rev. Fr. Leonard Feeney, M.I.C.M., *Bread of Life*, (Still River, MA: Saint Benedict Center, 1974) pp.97, 98.
[51] *Res sacramenti*=the grace signified and produced by the sacrament.
[52] *Ex ipso voto*, the very term used by the Council of Trent, thereby giving to St. Thomas Aquinas the approbation of an infallible Council. Some followers of Fr. Feeney claim that the Council of Trent did not uphold this teaching of St. Thomas on baptism of desire: Bro. Francis, "Reply to Verbum," *Res Fidei*, February 1987, p.9. We see here how false this claim is.

actual reception of this sacrament, a man can obtain salvation[53] through the desire of receiving it, just as he can obtain it before baptism through the desire of baptism, as stated above (*ibid.*)!

Yet there is a difference in two respects. First of all, because baptism is the beginning of the spiritual life, and the door of the sacraments, whereas the Eucharist is, as it were, the consummation of the spiritual life, and the end of all the sacraments, as was observed above: for by the hallowings of all the sacraments, preparation is made for receiving or consecrating the Eucharist. Consequently, the reception of baptism is necessary for starting the spiritual life, while the receiving of the Eucharist is requisite for its consummation, not for its simple possession; it is sufficient to have it in desire (*in voto*), as an end is possessed in desire and intention.

Another difference is because, by baptism, a man is ordained to the Eucharist, and therefore from the fact of children being baptized, they are destined by the Church to the Eucharist; and just as they believe through the Church's faith, so they desire the Eucharist through the Church's intention, and as a result, receive its reality. But they are not disposed for baptism by any previous sacrament, and consequently, before receiving baptism, in no way have they baptism in desire, which adults alone can have, consequently, infants cannot have the reality of the sacrament without receiving the sacrament (of baptism) itself. Therefore this sacrament (of Eucharist) is not necessary for salvation in the same way as baptism is.

You certainly have noticed in this text that the "desire" of the Holy Eucharist required by St. Thomas is an "implicit" desire in these baptized children.

Fr. Feeney puts aside this word of Our Lord, saying that the Eucharist is only of necessity of precept, not of means.[54] *St. Thomas rightfully teaches that, both in baptism and in the Eucharist, the reality of the sacrament (res sacramenti, i.e.,* the grace of the sacrament) is absolutely necessary: to have the life of Christ in us (grace of baptism) and to be united with the Mystical Body of Christ (grace of the Eucharist) are of the essence of salvation; however the exterior sacrament (*sacramentum tantum*) is necessary of a necessity of means,[55] as the normal mean for obtaining the grace of the sacrament.

---

[53] Note that St. Thomas speaks here of salvation itself, see p.98.
[54] Bro. Michael, letter of March 3, 1986.

THE SCRIPTURES TEACH BAPTISM OF BLOOD AND BAPTISM OF DESIRE

Indeed, the Fathers have always striven to be faithful to the *entire* Scriptures, not interpreting one passage and neglecting others, but holding the truth of the whole. There are quite a few other passages in the Scripture that support the traditional doctrine on Baptism of Blood and Baptism of Desire.

Our Lord Jesus Christ Himself taught baptism of blood: "I have a baptism wherewith I am to be baptized: and how am I straitened until it be accomplished?" (Lk. 12:50) and "Can you...be baptized with the baptism wherewith I am baptized? [...] and with the baptism wherewith I am baptized you shall be baptized" (Mk. 10:38,39). That makes eight times that Our Lord used the word *baptism* for baptism of blood. The triple repetition of the word *baptism* is a typical Hebraism to stress its importance. Our Lord Jesus Christ also used the word "baptism" to describe the fervor of the Holy Ghost, Whom the Apostles would receive at Pentecost: "For John indeed baptized with water, but you shall be baptized with the Holy Ghost, not many days hence" (Acts 1:5, see Acts 11:16). Thus in calling them "baptisms" we follow the example of Our Lord Jesus Christ Himself.

Our Lord Jesus Christ Himself taught baptism of desire, saying to the penitent thief: "Amen I say to thee: this day thou shalt be with me in paradise!" (Lk. 23:43). The penitent thief did not die because of his confession of the Faith (he died because of his thefts!), but he died confessing the Faith, which Our Lord deemed sufficient to go to Paradise! "Everyone therefore that shall confess me before men, I will also confess him before my Father who is in heaven" (Mt. 10:32). This example is given by the Fathers (Cyprian, Augustine); whatever reserve one can make on their interpretation, one thing remains certain: neither Our Lord nor the Fathers consider that the character of baptism was needed

---

[55] Something is necessary of a necessity of means to obtain a goal, when without it, there is no way that we can reach that goal; it is only a necessity of precept when we are commanded to do it though there is no intrinsic necessity: *e.g.,* not to eat meat on Fridays is only necessary of a necessity of precept for a good Christian life; however, eating is necessary of a necessity of means for life; yet God did grant certain saints such as St. Nicholas de Flüe to live for years without eating!

for the penitent thief, it was sufficient for him to die while confessing Our Lord. St. Augustine says in his *retractations* that we did not know whether he was baptized; indeed, yet he does not say that had he not been baptized, he would not have been saved.

Moreover, as one easily notices in reading the explanation of the Fathers and theologians on baptism of blood and baptism of desire, the Church has taught this doctrine in order to respect many other universal statements of Our Lord in the Scriptures. We ought to follow her example and remain faithful to all the words of Our Lord, in the same sense as the Church explains them.

Sometimes followers of Fr. Feeney object by quoting St. Paul saying: "one baptism" (Eph. 4:5). Here again, let us hear the Fathers of the Church. St. Jerome–the Doctor of the Holy Scripture–in his commentary of the Epistle to the Ephesians: "The One Baptism is also in water, in the Spirit and in the fire. Of which Our Lord also says: 'I have a baptism wherewith I am to be baptized' (Lk. 12:50) and elsewhere 'with the baptism wherewith I am baptized you shall be baptized' (Mk. 10:39)" (In Eph. 4, PL 26, 496). The same St. Paul speaks to the Hebrews of "the doctrine of baptisms" (Heb. 6:2), not referring to the many washings of the Old Testament, but rather to the steps of the Christian initiation! See how the Fathers are careful to respect the whole Holy Scripture, and do not distort one passage to a private interpretation that would neglect other passages.

St. Paul in that passage (Eph. 4:5) speaks of the unity of the Church, which is made of unity of government (one Lord), unity of faith (one Faith) and unity of worship (sacraments: one baptism). There is only one sacrament of baptism, the other two are not sacraments, though they are called "baptism" because by them Christ gives the grace of baptism, sanctifying grace, which is the one life that makes the unity of the Body of Christ. Thus one can also say that St. Paul's words apply to the one grace of baptism, which grace is the Life of Christ in us, also given in exceptional cases by baptism of blood and desire.

In conclusion, let us not introduce a private interpretation of the Holy Scripture in opposition to that of the Fathers, but rather "hold fast to the doctrine of the Fathers,"[56] Doctors, and popes.

The Authority of Popes and Councils

The followers of Fr. Feeney often quote three infallible[57] pronouncements of popes, *viz.*, Innocent III in the Fourth Lateran Council, Boniface VIII in *Unam Sanctam*, and Eugene IV in the Council of Florence. However, they misinterpret these definitions, by disregarding the teaching of the very same popes, sometimes within the very same council! And they disregard the teaching of other popes and councils. The root of their error is to think that baptism of blood and baptism of desire are incompatible with the dogma *Extra Ecclesiam nulla salus*. In no way does this dogma exclude baptism of blood and baptism of desire, as we shall see.

INNOCENT III AND THE FOURTH LATERAN COUNCIL

In 1215, this pope convoked this council against the Albigenses, *etc.*, and imposed on them a profession of faith which contains: "I believe firmly and profess simply that... there is one universal Church of the faithful, outside of which absolutely no one is saved..." (Dz. 430). Clearly he does not speak of baptism, but of belonging to the Church. The very same pope, a few years earlier, twice explicitly taught baptism of desire and approved the teaching of St. Augustine and St. Ambrose! Hence, one ought to conclude that this teaching is not opposed to the dogma.

Moreover, St. Thomas Aquinas and St. Bonaventure, two great doctors of the Church, were teaching explicitly the doctrine of baptism of blood and baptism of desire just a few years after this council; had this council meant a condemnation of this doctrine, they would certainly have been reproached for it by their adversaries, which was not the case. And they would never have been declared Doctors of the Church had they taught a doctrine

---

[56] Dz. 388, Pope Innocent III.
[57] It is not here the place to discuss whether they are infallible in virtue of the extra-ordinary magisterium, or in virtue of the ordinary magisterium. Let it be sufficient to agree that they are infallible.

against an already defined dogma. Hence one must conclude that this infallible pronouncement of Innocent III is not against Baptism of Blood and Baptism of Desire.

Here is the Pope's teaching:

> To your inquiry we respond thus: We assert without hesitation (on the authority of the holy Fathers Augustine and Ambrose) that the priest who, as you indicated (in your letter), **had died without the water of baptism**, because he persevered in the faith of holy mother the Church and in the confession of the name of Christ, was freed from original sin and attained the joy of the heavenly fatherhood. Read in the eighth book of Augustine's *City of God* where among other things it is written, "Baptism is ministered invisibly to one whom not contempt of religion but death excludes." Read again the book also of the blessed Ambrose concerning the death of Valentinian where he says the same thing. Therefore, to questions concerning the dead, **you should hold the opinions of the learned Fathers**, and in your church you should join in prayers and you should have sacrifice offered to God for the priest mentioned.[58]

These same last words perfectly apply to the disciples of Fr. Feeney.

Again the same Pope Innocent III teaches:

> You have, to be sure, intimated that a certain Jew, when at the point of death, since he lived only among Jews, immersed himself in water while saying: "I baptize myself in the name of the Father, and of the Son, and of the Holy Ghost. Amen." We respond that, since there should be a distinction between the one baptizing and the one baptized, as is clearly gathered from the words of the Lord, when he says to the Apostles: "Go, baptize all nations in the name *etc.*" [see Mt. 28:19], the Jew mentioned must be baptized again by another, that it may be shown that he who is baptized is one person, and he who baptizes another....If, however, such a one had died immediately, he would have rushed to his heavenly home without delay because of the faith of the sacrament, though not because of the sacrament of the Faith.[59]

---

[58] From the letter *Apostolicam Sedem* to the Bishop of Cremona, of uncertain time, Dz. 388.
[59] From the letter *Debitum Pastoralis officii* to the Bishop of Metz, Aug. 28, 1206, Dz. 413.

Thus, had he died, in spite of an invalid baptism, he would still have been saved *because of the faith of the sacrament.* Such is the teaching of Pope Innocent III, who did not consider such a soul outside the Church.

BONIFACE VIII: *UNAM SANCTAM*

The second text often referred to by the followers of Fr. Feeney is the bull *Unam Sanctam* of Pope Boniface VIII. Here is the text:

> We are compelled in virtue of our faith to believe and maintain that there is only one Catholic Church, and that one apostolic. This we firmly believe and profess without qualification. Outside this Church there is no salvation and no remission of sins. [...] Further we declare, say, define, and pronounce that it is absolutely necessary for the salvation of every human creature to be subject to the Roman Pontiff (Dz. 468, 469).

Since baptism of desire as defined by St. Thomas (in conformity with the whole Tradition) includes the remission of sin, and baptism of blood forgives all sin and all penalty due to sin, it follows logically according to the above principle taught by Pope Boniface that such persons do belong to the Catholic Church, though their bond is not complete.

Indeed the essential bond with Our Lord Jesus Christ and His Church is sanctifying grace, a share in the life of Christ, which can only be had within the Body of Christ; the character of baptism is not the essential bond, it can be had outside the Church, and all the souls of the saints of the Old Testament are in heaven without that character. It is a *sign* of the belonging to Christ, not *the belonging itself*; it is a source of grace for the faithful in the Church, but denounces the unfaithful outside the Church.

As for the submission to the Roman Pontiff, it is explicit in the catechumens who die for the Faith of Peter. It is also in those catechumens who receive faithfully the instructions in the Faith of Peter and out of obedience to the authorities of the Church wait for the appointed day of their baptism: if an accident happens to them, their submission to the Roman Pontiff is undeniable. It is the common teaching that this subjection exists also, though it may be only implicit, in those who have charity, but whose knowledge of the Faith is limited without fault on their part: indeed "charity is not puffed up" (I Cor. 13:4), it is obedient to the Law of Christ (Jn 14:21), this disposition of humility and obedience to the order set by Christ includes virtually the submission to the Roman Pontiff.

EUGENE IV AND THE COUNCIL OF FLORENCE

Perhaps the clearest definition of the dogma *Outside the Church there is no salvation* is given on February 4, 1442, by the Council of Florence, which intended the union with the Greeks, Armenians and Jacobites.

> [The holy Roman Church] firmly believes, professes, and preaches that "no one remaining outside the Catholic Church, not just pagans, but also Jews or heretics or schismatics, can become partakers of eternal life; but they will go to the 'everlasting fire which was prepared for the devil and his angels' (Mt. 25:41), unless before the end of life they are joined to the Church. For union with the body of the Church is of such importance that the sacraments of the Church are helpful to salvation only for those remaining in it; and fasts, almsgiving, other works of piety, and the exercise of Christian warfare bear eternal rewards for them alone. And no one can be saved, no matter how much alms he has given, even if he sheds his blood for the name of Christ, unless he remains in the bosom and the unity of the Catholic Church."[60]

Some followers of Fr. Feeney, reading the last sentence, pretend that it is a condemnation of Baptism of Blood.[61] This only shows their ignorance of the fact that this whole paragraph is a quote by the Council of Florence of a passage of St. Fulgentius, in his book *On Faith, to Peter*.[62] Now, when a Pope or a Council quote a Father of the Church, they certainly do not give another meaning to his words than this Father gave. Now, just a few pages before, the same St. Fulgentius in that same book said:

> Hold most firmly, and have absolutely no doubt, that, apart from those who are baptized in their blood for the name of Christ, no man shall receive eternal life, who has not been converted here below from his evils by penance and has not been freed by the sacrament of faith and penance, *i.e.*, by Baptism.[63]

---

[60] Dz. 714.

From the moment when our Savior said: "Unless one is born again from water and the Holy Ghost, he cannot enter in the kingdom of God," no one can enter the kingdom of heaven nor receive eternal life without the sacrament of baptism, except those who, *without baptism, shed their blood for Christ in the Catholic Church.* Whoever receives the sacrament of baptism in the name of the Father and of the Son and of the Holy Ghost, either in the Catholic Church or in whatever sect, receives indeed the integral sacrament; but he shall not have salvation, which is the virtue of the sacrament, if he receives the sacrament outside of the Catholic Church. Therefore, he must return to the Catholic Church, not in order to receive again the sacrament of baptism, which no one may reiterate in any baptized person, but in order that he receive eternal life in the Catholic communion; because no one remaining outside of the Catholic Church with the sacrament of baptism is ever capable to receive this eternal life.[64]

This text beautifully shows that the Fathers always gave the greater importance to the "virtue of the sacrament," *i.e.,* the grace of baptism, the life of the soul, rather than to the character of the

---

[61] For instance, Mr. Thomas A. Hutchinson, *Desire and Deception*, p.47. This book contains real heresy, such as: "Just as the Holy Ghost had existed from all eternity, so too had the Son, the divine *Logos*, although not yet incarnate. *Similarly* from all eternity was Our Lady present in the mind of God as the figure of Wisdom....Prior to their respective *incarnations*, the *Logos*, Holy Wisdom and the Church acted and worked in an invisible manner, afterwards Christ, Our Lady and the Church were visible and active" (pp.16, 20). From this one gathers that as Christ is the Incarnated *Logos*, so is Our Lady the *Incarnated* Holy Wisdom and the Church is the Incarnated Idea of the Church. Now this is heresy! Has Our Lady two natures in one person??? Mixing superficial erudition with so many false statements, that book is really *deceiving*: For instance: "We know that it was the rule for Christians in prison to be baptized soon upon entrance therein to prepare them for death; it is from such accounts, for example, that we know that infants were baptized, although outside of jail baptism was generally deferred until adulthood" (p.23). This is completely false! I have never seen such "rule," but have rather read St. Cyprian's Epistle No. 64, telling that the bishops of the Council of Carthage which he presided had *unanimously* agreed not to wait until the 8th day, but that the children ought to be baptized within two or three days, and Origen telling us that it was a tradition from the Apostles themselves.
[62] *De Fide, ad Petrum*, 38, 78 *sqq.*, R.J., No.2275.
[63] *De Fide, ad Petrum*, 38, 30. P.L. 65, Col.702.
[64] *De Fide, ad Petrum*, 3, 41. R.J., No.2269.

sacrament: they believed that this grace of the sacrament can be received even without the sacrament itself, and that some saints did die with that grace though without the sacrament, as in the case of martyrs (which was the most common at their time).

From that text, it is quite clear that a Catholic catechumen dying for Christ before his baptism was saved, and was considered *in the Catholic Church*. When St. Fulgentius, a few paragraphs later, speaks of those who shed their blood for Christ outside the Church, he speaks of heretics or schismatics, not of catechumens.[65]

Moreover, the very Council of Florence, in the very same decree for the Jacobites (part of the bull *Cantate Domino*) mentions baptism of desire! Here is the passage:

> As for children, because of the danger of death, which can happen often, since **no other remedy is available for them besides the sacrament of Baptism**, by which they are delivered from the domination of the devil and adopted as children of God, [the Council] warns that one ought not to delay the sacred Baptism for 40 or 80 days or another time according to certain customs, but it should rather be conferred as soon as fittingly possible.[66]

Now the underlined passage is a quote from St. Thomas Aquinas. Knowing how closely the Council of Florence followed St. Thomas's teaching, it is undoubtedly a confirmation by the very Council of Florence of St. Thomas's teaching. Now here is the whole text of St. Thomas:

Whether Baptism should be deferred?
(*Summa Theologica,* III, Q.68, A.3)

> I answer that, In this matter we must make a distinction and see whether those who are to be baptized are children or adults. For if they be children, Baptism should not be deferred. First, because in them we do not look for better instruction or fuller conversion. Secondly, because of the danger of death, for *no other remedy is available for them besides the sacrament of Baptism*.
> On the other hand, *adults have a remedy in the mere desire for Baptism*, as stated above (A.2, see p.73). And therefore Bap-

---

[65] See another example of the clear distinction that the Fathers were making between both in St. Cyprian (p.58).
[66] Dz. 712.

tism should not be conferred on adults as soon as they are converted, but it should be deferred until some fixed time. First, as a safeguard to the Church, lest she be deceived through baptizing those who come to her under false pretenses, according to I Jn. 4:1: "Believe not every spirit, but try the spirits, if they be of God." And those who approach Baptism are put to this test, when their faith and morals are subjected to proof for a space of time. Secondly, this is needful as being useful for those who are baptized; for they require a certain space of time in order to be fully instructed in the faith, and to be drilled in those things that pertain to the Christian mode of life. Thirdly, a certain reverence for the sacrament demands a delay whereby men are admitted to Baptism at the principal festivities, *viz.* of Easter and Pentecost, the result being that they receive the sacrament with greater devotion.

There are, however, two reasons for forgoing this delay. First, when those who are to be baptized appear to be perfectly instructed in the faith and ready for Baptism; thus, Philip baptized the Eunuch at once (Acts 8); and Peter, Cornelius and those who were with him (Acts 10). Secondly, by reason of sickness or some kind of danger of death. Wherefore Pope Leo says (Epist. xvi): "Those who are threatened by death, sickness, siege, persecution, or shipwreck, should be baptized at any time." Yet if a man is forestalled by death, so as to have no time to receive the sacrament, while he awaits the season appointed by the Church, he is saved, yet "so as by fire," as stated above (A.2, ad 2). Nevertheless he sins if he defer being baptized beyond the time appointed by the Church, except this be for an unavoidable cause and with the permission of the authorities of the Church. But even this sin, with his other sins, can be washed away by his subsequent contrition, which takes the place of Baptism, as stated above (Q.66, A.11).

In his usual custom, St. Thomas is very clear. But the simple look at this passage shows that "the other remedy" in the sentence of the Council of Florence refers to Baptism of Desire! Thus far from being against Baptism of Desire, the very Council of Florence, the very bull *Cantate Domino,* teaches it as being "another remedy" permitting a delay for adult catechumens for the reasons given by St. Thomas. And lest some follower of Fr. Feeney say that this passage is not *infallible*, let him consider that the paragraph on baptism from which it is taken starts with the very same words as the one on the Church: "[The holy Roman Church] firmly believes, professes, and teaches that..." Hence both paragraphs have the very same degree of authority.

COUNCIL OF TRENT

As the Council of Florence made its own St. Thomas's teaching on Baptism of Desire, so did the Council of Trent. The very famous expression *"re aut voto*–in deed or in desire"[67] was used twice by the Council of Trent, once in the explanation ("chapter") explicitly applied to the necessity of baptism and once even in an *ex cathedra* canon on the very necessity of sacraments in general. Here are the texts of the Council:

> Session 6, Chapter 4: Justification is a passing from the state in which man is born a son of the first Adam, to the state of grace and adoption as sons of God (see Rom. 8:15) through the second Adam, Jesus Christ our Savior. After the promulgation of the gospel this passing cannot take place without the water of regeneration *or the desire for it*, as it is written: "Unless a man be born again of water and the Holy Ghost, he cannot enter into the kingdom of God" (Jn. 3:5).
>
> Session 7, Canon 4 : If anyone says that the sacraments of the New Law are not necessary for salvation, but that they are superfluous; and that men can, without the sacraments *or the desire of them*, obtain the grace of justification by faith alone, although it is true that not all the sacraments are necessary for each individual, let him be anathema (Dz. 847).

These texts are so strong an approval of the doctrine of baptism of desire that a doctor of the Church, St. Alphonsus Liguori, states that "it is *de fide* that there are some men *saved* by baptism of desire" and explicitly refers to these texts to support his affirmation.

However, the followers of Fr. Feeney try to escape the Council's doctrine by a false reasoning. In a leaflet entitled *Desire, Justification and Salvation at the Council of Trent* put out by Saint Benedict Center, they set their reasoning in five points[68]:

> *1)* The Catholic Faith is the foundation of all justification. [Session 6, Chapter 6, 7, 8] *2)* A person who has the Catholic Faith can attain the state of justification[69] if that person receives

---

[67] *ST*, III, Q.68, A.2, see p.73.

the Sacraments or has the resolve (desire) to receive them. [Session 6, Chapter 4, Session 7, Canon 4] *3)* The reception of the Sacraments is required for Salvation. [Session 6, Chapter 7; Session 7, Canon 4, 5, 2] *4)* In conclusion, justification can be attained by a person with the Catholic Faith together with at least a desire for the Sacraments. He cannot attain Salvation unless he receives the Sacraments.[70]

One can easily see a first flaw in their reasoning in that they quote the same Canon 4 of Session 7 (see above) for both point *2)* and point *3)*: now if one says that *the sacraments **or the desire of them*** are necessary for justification, it is clear that such a one says that they are also necessary for salvation, since there is no salvation without first justification, and hence such a one does not fall under the first part of the canon. Indeed, whoever says that the sacraments are superfluous does not really desire them!

But the major flaw of their reasoning is to consider only one kind of necessity, as if the Church had never taught distinctions between absolute necessity, necessity of means (which God can bypass), and necessity of precept. Hence they build a false syllogism:

---

[68] They say, "five points," but in fact their "fourth" point is a summary of the first three. Their fifth point is not part of the reasoning. This fifth point is: "No Pope, Council, or theologian says that *baptism of desire* is a sacrament. Likewise, no Pope, Council or theologian says that *baptism of desire* incorporates one into the Catholic Church." The first sentence is true. The second is false; see p.106.

[69] *Sic!* As quoted above, the Council of Trent defines justification as "a passing"; the followers of Fr. Feeney often speak of it as a "state." This is not consistent with the Council's teaching.

[70] We give here only the title of the sections and the references which they quote under each title. The relevant references are found in the text here above or below. Sess. 6, Chap. 6, 7, 8 do not touch the problem. One must note a misleading translation at the end of that Sess. 6, Chap. 8: "the instrumental cause [of justification] is the sacrament of baptism, which is the sacrament of faith, without which no man was ever justified." This leads the reader to think that the Council teaches that without the sacrament no man was ever justified; no, the pronoun "which" refers to faith in Latin and not to "sacrament"; the true meaning is: "without the faith no man was ever justified." Notice carefully the way the Council phrased its teaching, in order that the absolute necessity would grammatically fall on *faith* and not on *sacrament*.

[Session 7] "Can. 5. If anyone says that baptism is optional, that is, not necessary for salvation, let him be anathema. Can. 2: If anyone says that true and natural water is not necessary for baptism and thus twists into some metaphor the words of our Lord Jesus Christ: 'unless a man be born again of water and the Holy Ghost', let him be anathema." In terms of a syllogism we have the infallible major premise: "Baptism is necessary for salvation," the infallible minor premise: "True and natural water is necessary for Baptism," and the infallible conclusion: "True and natural water is necessary for salvation!"

The answer is simple: of *what kind* of necessity does the Council speak in Canon 5? Of the same of which the Council of Trent itself has spoken in Session 6, Chapter 4, and again in Session 7, Canon 4, *i.e.,* a necessity *re aut voto*—in deed or in desire. Their syllogism hence become: baptism is necessary *re aut voto* for salvation; now true and natural water is necessary for baptism (it belongs to its essence); hence true and natural water is necessary *re aut voto* for salvation! To say that baptism of water is *necessary in fact or in desire* is clearly not to say that it is superfluous, nor unnecessary for salvation!

See later p.98 for a discussion of *justification* versus *salvation*.

Pius IX

Pius IX is the Pope of the *Syllabus* and of the definition of papal infallibility. In one of his encyclicals from which propositions of the *Syllabus* were drawn, on August 10, 1863, he wrote:

> And here, Beloved Sons and Venerable Brethren, it is necessary once more to mention and censure the serious error into which some Catholics have unfortunately fallen. For they are of the opinion that men who live in errors, estranged from the true faith and from Catholic unity, can attain eternal life. That is in direct opposition to Catholic teaching. We all know that those who are afflicted with invincible ignorance with regard to our holy religion, if they carefully keep the precepts of the natural law that have been written by God in the hearts of all men, if they are prepared to obey God, and if they lead a virtuous and dutiful life, can attain eternal life by the power of divine light and grace. For God, who reads comprehensively in every detail the minds and souls, the thoughts and habits of all men, will not permit, in accordance with his infinite goodness and mercy, anyone who is not guilty of a voluntary fault to suffer eternal pun-

ishment. However, also well-known is the Catholic dogma that no one can be saved outside the Catholic Church, and that those who obstinately oppose the authority and definitions of that Church, and who stubbornly remain separated from the unity of the Church and from the successor of Peter, the Roman Pontiff (to whom the Savior has entrusted the care of his vineyard), cannot obtain salvation.[71]

Fr. Feeney himself belittles this papal teaching:

> ...one or two carelessly worded sentences in an encyclical of Pope Pius IX...An incidental sentence in a letter of Pope Pius IX...a lengthy letter which was devoid of the chastity of Papal infallible pronouncement...[72]

This kind of treatment of a blessed Pope, great adversary of the Liberals, as soon as he says one word against their false thesis, is something we will see again and again, with sadness, among the followers of Fr. Feeney when they deal with any Father, Doctor or ecclesiastical writer that goes against them. This is no proper argument!

This passage of Pope Pius IX shows clearly: *1)* baptism of desire is not opposed to the dogma *outside the Catholic Church there is no salvation, 2)* baptism of desire is not without *divine light and grace, i.e.,* sanctifying grace, which includes faith and charity, *3)* baptism of desire is incompatible with indifference to God, to religion, to resistance to the Catholic Church.

Pope Pius IX is famous for having convoked the First Vatican Council. He had asked trusted theologians to prepares *Schemas, i.e.,* drafts to be studied by the Council fathers. These schemas teach the commonly taught Catholic doctrine; though they do not have the same authority as the promulgated chapters nor the

---

[71] *Quanto conficiamur moerore*, Dz. 1677, *The Church Teaches*, No.178.

[72] *Bread of Life*, p.53. Catherine Goddard Clarke, in *The Loyolas and the Cabots*, p.237, has similar belittling language: "Because of three or four **weak** sentences in his encyclicals, Pope Pius IX had left dogmatic utterance **unsafeguarded, unprotected**, and the only thing the Liberals quote from him are the three or four well-chosen sentences that serve their purposes. It is through ill-will that the Liberals do this, but, again, if we may respectfully say so, Pope Pius IX **should have seen** this when he made the statements. Pope Pius IX sensed somewhat that he had spoken occasionally **unguardedly...**" It does not occur to them that Pope Pius IX may have been right, and that they are those who should correct themselves!

canons of the First Vatican Council, they still express the *ordinary magisterium*. Here is the text of the relevant passages:

> Title VII: Outside of the Church no one can be saved. Furthermore, it is a dogma of faith that no one can be saved outside the Church. Nevertheless, those who are invincibly ignorant of Christ and His Church are not to be judged worthy of eternal punishment because of this ignorance. For they are innocent in the eyes of the Lord of any fault in this matter. God wishes all men to be saved and to come to a knowledge of the truth; if one does what he can, God does not withhold the grace from him to obtain justification and eternal life. But no one obtains eternal life if he dies separated from the unity of faith or from communion with the Church through his own fault....
>
> Canon V: if anyone says that the Church of Christ is not a society absolutely necessary for eternal salvation, or that men can be saved by the practice of any religion whatsoever, let him be anathema!
>
> Canon XIII: if anyone says that the true Church of Christ, outside of which no one can be saved, is other than the Roman Church, one, holy, catholic and apostolic, let him be anathema![73]

Now Bro. Robert Mary (*op. cit.*, p.171) calls the writers of this *schema* "liberal periti" and comments: "This is the same imprecise language that Pius IX used earlier in his pontificate." By his own words Bro. Robert Mary condemns himself: he acknowledges that these theologians used "the same language as Pius IX," so they do not speak in their own name, but express the Pope's teaching! Bro. Robert Mary continues to belittle this *schema*, forgetting that much of it was taken again by Pope Pius XII in *Mystici Corporis*.

St. Pius X

In his *Catechism*, Pope St. Pius X teaches:

Question: Can the absence of Baptism be supplied in any other way?

---

[73] *L'Eglise,* appendix pp.7*, 16*, 17*, collection of pontifical documents on the Church prepared by the monks of Solesmes. See also *The Church Teaches*, No.196, p.91.

Answer: The absence of Baptism can be supplied by martyrdom, which is called the Baptism of Blood, or by an act of perfect love of God, or of contrition, along with the desire, at least implicit, of Baptism, and this is called Baptism of Desire.[74]

BENEDICT XV

St. Pius X had decided the great work to bring all the laws of the Church together into one Code of Canon Law; he had the work far advanced when death prevented him from finalizing it. Pope Benedict XV published it. This work has a very great authority, since it presents the practical expression of the Catholic Faith as applied in its laws.

The definition of baptism is a marvel of conciseness and theological precision:

> Canon 737, §1. Baptism, the door and foundation of the Sacraments, in fact or at least in desire necessary unto salvation for all, is not validly conferred except through the ablution of true and natural water with the prescribed form of words.

Note that it speaks of necessity unto salvation, not merely unto justification. And the Canon Law draws the consequence for burial:

> Canon 1239, §1. Those who died without baptism should not be admitted to the ecclesiastical burial.
>
> §2. The catechumens who with no fault of their own die without baptism, should be treated as the baptized.

The Authority of the Fathers

THE ROMAN MARTYROLOGY[75]

> January 23: At Rome, St. Emerentiana, a Virgin and Martyr. She was just a catechumen when she was stoned by the Gentiles while praying on the tomb of St. Agnes, who was her foster-sister.

---

[74] *Catechism of St. Pius X,* Instauratio Press, p.71. (Available from Angelus Press.)

[75] Bro. Robert Mary (*op. cit.*, pp.172-192) spends twenty pages rewriting the history of these martyrs, implicitly accusing St. Bede or St. Paulinus and others of lying.

April 12: At Braga in Portugal, the martyr St. Victor, who, although only a catechumen, refused to adore an idol, and confessed Jesus Christ with great constancy. After suffering many torments, he was beheaded, and thus merited to be baptized in his own blood.

June 22: At Verulam in England, in the time of Diocletian, St. Alban, martyr, who gave himself up in order to save a cleric whom he had harbored. After being scourged and subjected to bitter torments, he was sentenced to capital punishment. With him also suffered one of the soldiers who led him to execution, for he was converted to Christ on the way and merited to be baptized in his own blood. St. Bede the Venerable has left an account of the noble combat of St. Alban and his companion.

It is to be noted here that St. Alban's life is given to us by St. Bede: who would dare to call St. Bede a liar? Now here are the words of St. Bede: "The soldier who had been moved by divine intuition to refuse to slay God's confessor was beheaded at the same time as Alban. And although *he had not received the purification of baptism*, there was no doubt that he was cleansed by the shedding of his own blood, and rendered fit to enter the kingdom of heaven."[76]

June 28: At Alexandria, in the persecution of Severus, the holy martyrs Plutarch, Serenus, Heraclides a catechumen, Heron a neophyte, another Serenus, Rháis a catechumen, Potamioena, and Marcella her mother...

Moreover in the Roman Breviary for the Feast of St. Martina, it was noted: "Several among her torturers, struck by the novelty of the miracle and drawn by the grace of Christ, embraced the Faith, and after torments deserved the glorious palm of martyrdom by decapitation" (Matins, Jan. 30, 5th lesson).

Fr. Ribadénéira mentions on May 24: "The persecution started very furiously in the city of Nantes, which was the cause for which Rogatian did not receive baptism, the priests having departed from the city; but the lack of the water of baptism was abundantly supplied by the effusion of his blood in martyrdom."[77]

---

[76] *History of the English Church and People,* Penguin 1955, p.47.
[77] *La Fleur des Saints,* (life of the saints for each day of the year) Vol.5, pp.386, 387.

Fr. Ribadénéira quotes St. Paulinus of Nola for his report of the life of St. Genesius, court's clerk of Arles[78] in France:

> When an impious and sacrilegious edict was read...he stood up, threw his registers at the feet of the judge, and renounced for ever his ministry....He fled from town to town....However, thinking he needed to be strengthened in the faith by baptism, not being yet reborn of the water and the Holy Ghost, he asked for it from the bishop through some trusted friends. But either the bishop had been himself arrested in the meantime, or fearing the youth of Genesius he did not want to put the sacrament in danger; anyhow, the bishop differed the sacrament, and bid him that the shedding of his blood for Jesus Christ would take place of the baptism he had so ardently desired....His executioners took his life by the sword.

FATHERS ON BAPTISM OF BLOOD

Tertullian (end of 2nd century)

> We have indeed a second font, one with the former: namely, that of blood, of which the Lord says: "I am to be baptized with a baptism" when He had already been baptized....This is the Baptism which **replaces that of the fountain, when it has not been received**, and restores it when it has been lost [*i.e.*, if, after baptism, one had fallen into sin, it restores to grace and thus salvation].[79]

---

[78] Feast August 25, Vol.VIII, p.440 *sqq*. Bro. Robert Mary's commentary runs thus: "Let us extract the important essentials from these two testimonies. The *Martyrology* informs us that Genesius 'declared himself a Christian.' *That means* he was already a baptized member of the Church. Fr. Butler tells us he was also a catechumen. *Therefore*, we know he was a baptized Catholic still undergoing instruction in a catechumenate. Both sources report that he was apprehended and beheaded, the Martyrology properly concluding that he 'attained to the glory of martyrdom through baptism in his own blood.' Here is a perfect example of what 'baptism of blood' really means. It applies *only* to the martyrdom of a baptized Catholic" (*op. cit.* p.190). One needs just to read St. Paulinus of Nola given above to see how far from the truth this apparent *logic* can lead the followers of Fr. Feeney! Instead of rewriting history, making liars of the saints who gave us accounts of these holy lives, and rewriting the doctrine of the Church to their liking, let them simply believe the accounts given by the saints and the doctrine it contains!

[79] *De Baptismo*, 16, 1, R.J., No. 309.

St. Cyril of Jerusalem:

> If any one does not receive baptism, he shall not be saved, except the martyrs, who even without the water shall receive the kingdom.[80]

St. John Chrysostom:

> Do not wonder that I called martyrdom a baptism: indeed there too the Spirit comes with much abundance, and works there the remission of sins and a wonderful and astonishing purification of the soul; and as those who are baptized by waters [are washed], so those who suffer martyrdom are washed in their own blood.[81]

St. Gregory Nazianzen, Orat. 39, *In Sancta Lumina,* 17; P.G. 35, 356.

> I know also a Fourth Baptism (besides that of Moses, John, and Jesus)—that by Martyrdom and blood, which also Christ Himself underwent;—and this one is far more august than all the others, inasmuch as it cannot be defiled by after-stains.

St. Paulinus of Nola: see on p.56 the account of St. Genesius's martyrdom.

St. Fulgentius (see p.45).

St. Bede the Venerable: see above his account of St. Alban's martyrdom. The followers of Fr. Feeney rewrite his account, saying that St. Alban baptized his companion; even without considering that they make of St. Bede a liar, the least they can say is that St. Bede the Venerable believed in the possibility of baptism of blood!

ST. CYPRIAN (3RD CENTURY)

St. Cyprian was Bishop of Carthage from 249 to 258; thus he went through three persecutions, that of Decius in 250, of Gallus in 253, and of Valerian in 257. He died in this persecution on September 14, 258. His writings are rich in doctrine, but he is especially renowned for his contention with Pope St. Stephen on whether to rebaptize the converts from heresy. The Pope stood by the traditional practice of not rebaptizing: "*nihil innovetur nisi*

---

[80] R.J., No. 811.
[81] R.J., No. 1139.

quod traditum est–let nothing be innovated, except that which is transmitted [by Tradition]."⁸² St. Cyprian stood by a local practice recently introduced in northern Africa which did rebaptize: his reasoning was that outside the Church there can be no salvation and no remission of sin; hence converts who were baptized in heresy never had received the remission of their sins, and therefore never had the new life of baptism. Hence the need of this first washing. This is the context of his letter No. 73 to Jubaianus.

This is the oldest testimony by a saint on the dogma *Outside the Church there is no salvation*. Immediately, St. Cyprian gives the doctrine on Baptism of Blood and Baptism of Desire as required for the proper understanding of the dogma. Here is the whole passage, so as to grasp the context:

> §21. Can the power of baptism be greater or of more avail than confession, than suffering, when one confesses Christ before men and is baptized in his own blood? And yet even this baptism does not benefit a heretic, although he has confessed Christ, and been put to death outside the Church, unless the patrons and advocates of heretics declare that the heretics who are slain in a false confession of Christ are martyrs, and assign to them the glory and the crown of martyrdom contrary to the testimony of the apostle, who says that it will profit them nothing although they were burnt and slain (I Cor. 13:3). But if not even the baptism of a public confession and blood can profit a heretic unto salvation, because there is no salvation out of the Church, how much less shall it be of advantage to him, if in a hiding-place and a cave of robbers, stained with the contagion of adulterous water,⁸³ he has not only not put off his old sins, but rather heaped up still newer and greater ones! Wherefore baptism cannot be common⁸⁴ to us and to heretics, to whom neither God the Father, nor Christ the Son, nor the Holy Ghost, nor the faith, nor the Church itself, is common. And therefore it behooves those to be baptized who come from heresy to the Church, that so they who are prepared, in the lawful, and true,

---

[82] Quoted by St. Cyprian in his Epistle No. 74, 1 (BAC, p.693).

[83] Baptism of water by the heretics: because of the obex of the wrong faith, it does not give sanctifying grace, but on the contrary, it adds a sacrilege, being the thievery of a sacrament.

[84] Later, the Church stated this teaching with more precision: baptism of water can be valid inside and outside the Church, but it cannot be fruitful outside the Church.

and only baptism of the holy Church, by divine regeneration, for the kingdom of God, may be born of both sacraments, because it is written, "Except a man be born of water and of the Spirit, he cannot enter into the kingdom of God" (Jn 3:5).

§22. On which place some, as if by human reasoning they were able to make void the truth of the Gospel declaration, object to us the case of catechumens; asking if any one of these, *before he is baptized in the Church*, should be apprehended and slain on confession of the name [of Christ], whether he would lose the hope of salvation and the reward of confession, because he had not previously been born again of water? Let men of this kind, who are aiders and favorers of heretics, know therefore, first, that those catechumens hold the sound faith and truth of the Church, and advance from the divine camp to do battle with the devil, with a full and sincere acknowledgment of God the Father, and of Christ, and of the Holy Ghost; then, that they certainly are not deprived of the sacrament[85] of baptism who are baptized with the most glorious and greatest baptism of blood, concerning which the Lord also said, that He had "another baptism to be baptized with" (Lk. 12:50). But the same Lord declares in the Gospel, that those who are baptized in their own blood, and sanctified by suffering, are perfected, and obtain the grace of the divine promise, when He speaks to the thief believing and confessing in His very passion, and promises that he should be with Himself in paradise. Wherefore we who are set over the faith and truth ought not to deceive and mislead those who come to the faith and truth, and repent, and beg that their sins should be remitted to them; but to instruct them when corrected by us, and reformed for the kingdom of heaven by celestial discipline.

§23. But some one says, "What, then, shall become of those who in past times, coming from heresy to the Church, were received without baptism?" The Lord is able by His mercy to give indulgence, and not to separate from the gifts of His Church those who by simplicity were admitted into the Church, and in the Church have fallen asleep.

St. Cyprian's reasoning in §21 is thus: one cannot have charity outside the Church (one cannot love Christ without loving His Church); now according to St. Paul, without charity the shedding

---

[85] Here, taken in the sense of "mystery": they are truly "born again," by the washing of their sins in their dying for Christ. He does not say here that baptism of blood gives a sacramental character.

of blood is of no avail to salvation; therefore there is no true martyrdom outside the Church, as St. Fulgentius, quoted by the Council of Florence, said. Now since such baptism of blood for Christ has more power unto sanctification than baptism of water, and yet outside the Church it cannot save, it follows that baptism of water outside the Church cannot save. Who does not see that this earliest testimony in favor of the dogma *Outside the Church there is no salvation* is completely distorted from its meaning if one denies baptism of blood?

In §22 St. Cyprian was most explicit about baptism of blood, and founded his doctrine on several passages of the Gospel.

In §23 we find a typical case of baptism of desire; this is the oldest testimony on this topic. St. Cyprian considered what to think of those converts baptized outside the Church and received in the Church only with the sacrament of penance without rebaptism. According to his opinion, they had an invalid baptism. Though this was not the case in the early Church when even the heretics were baptizing properly, it can happen today; indeed in former days the Church considered that, for the certitude of the sacrament, given the fact that some Protestant sects were not baptizing properly, we ought to rebaptize conditionally except if the proof was made of the validity of the first baptism. But, out of ecumenism, the presumption has now been turned around (not to rebaptize unless one has the proof of invalidity); hence the door is opened to cases where converts from Protestantism who really had an invalid baptism are received without being baptized. So what happens to them? They have the Catholic faith, live "with simplicity" and "have fallen asleep in the Church," yet without a valid baptism! St. Cyprian gave then the very same answer which will be always given by the Fathers and Doctors after him: "*Potens est Deus misericordia sua*–God is powerful in His Mercy" to save them! This passage is quoted by St. Robert Bellarmine: thus far from being disapproved by the Church, the Fathers on this point of doctrine have been constantly approved by her.

Note that St. Cyprian considered both to be in the Church: the Catholic catechumen martyrs "advance from the divine camp," *i.e.*, they go to the battle against the persecutor as belonging to the Army of Christ, the Church! And the men with baptism of desire "fall asleep in the Church."

St. Ambrose (3rd century)

The Empress Justina was Arian and had violently opposed St. Ambrose. At her death in 388, her young son Valentinian II was given in the care of the Catholic emperor Theodosius; he became a Catholic catechumen. In May 392, he wrote to St. Ambrose, begging him to come and see him in Vienne (France). "Come and give me Baptism, before my expedition against the barbarians!" But his military officer Arbogast had him assassinated, and sent his dead body to Milan![86] St. Ambrose preached for the burial:

> But I hear you lamenting because he had not received the sacraments of Baptism. Tell me, what else could we have, except the will to it, the asking for it? He too had just now this desire; and after he came into Italy it was begun, and a short time ago he signified that he wished to be baptized by me. Did he, then, not have the grace which he desired? Did he not have what he eagerly sought? Certainly, because he sought it, he received it (see Mt. 7:7). Otherwise, why would it be written: "But the just man, if he be prevented with death, shall be in rest (Wis. 4:7)?"[87]

Note how St. Ambrose based his teaching on the Scriptures, as do all the Fathers and Doctors. So much so for those who pretend that baptism of blood or of desire have "no scriptural foundation."[88]

Though very small in itself, this text of St. Ambrose is very important because it is quoted approvingly by almost every single Doctor or theologian (even Pope Innocent III) when speaking on Baptism of Desire.

Sometimes the followers of Fr. Feeney belittle this passage: "with Baptism, he [Fr. Feeney] found it necessary to improve upon the teaching of some of the Doctors....Their words of assurance to worried catechumens can hardly be lifted up as part of the deposit of faith."[89] If this were true, then the Fathers were giving a *false* "assurance to worried catechumens"! But to deny the explicit teaching of the Fathers and the Doctors, that is not *to improve* on them, but rather to be unfaithful to them. In another letter, the

---

[86] Fr. F. Mourret, *Histoire Générale de l'Eglise*, p.328.
[87] R.J., No.1328.
[88] *Desire and Deception*, p.23.
[89] Bro. Michael, MICM, letter of 3rd March 1986, p.6.

same one writes: "Of course the circumstances of this oration must be taken into consideration. He was speaking at the funeral of the Emperor who was his friend. Was that a proper place for clarifying a dogma?...St. Ambrose may have meant that Valentinian got what he prayed for and was baptized by one of his servants."[90] Does he infer that St. Ambrose was ashamed of and watered down the dogma in such an occasion? If the Emperor would have been "baptized by one of his servants," the word of it would certainly have gone around and reached St. Ambrose, who would not have missed the occasion to point this out! His very use of the words "prevented by death" rather exclude this interpretation. But remember, he was assassinated: what assassin is likely either to give his intended victim sufficient warning to arrange for a hasty baptism or to himself perform such an act of charity for the object of his murderous intentions?

ST. AUGUSTINE (4TH CENTURY)

St Augustine, in his very treatise on baptism, writes this:

> I do not hesitate to put the Catholic catechumen, burning with divine love, before a baptized heretic. Even within the Catholic Church herself, we put the good catechumen ahead of the wicked baptized person. Nor do we hereby do any injury to the Sacrament of Baptism, which the former has not yet received, while the latter has it already. Nor do we think that the catechumen's sacrament[91] is to be preferred to the Sacrament of Baptism, just because we recognize that a specified catechumen may be better and more faithful than a specified baptized person. The centurion Cornelius (Acts 10), not yet baptized, was better than Simon (Acts 8:9-24) already baptized. For Cornelius, even before his Baptism, was filled up with the Holy Ghost, while Simon, even after his Baptism, was puffed up with an unclean spirit. Cornelius, however, would have been convicted of contempt for so holy a sacrament, if, even after he had received the Holy Ghost, he had refused to be baptized.[92]

---

[90] Bro. Michael, letter to Dr. Coomaraswamy, February 2, 1983.
[91] The tasting of salt, symbolizing purity and incorruption, is what was termed the Catechumen's sacrament. It is at the beginning of the rite of baptism for infants, but for adults it was and still may be given in stages.
[92] *De Baptismo*, IV, 21, 28; R.J., No.1630, BAC, p.558.

Notice how St. Augustine considers the catechumen as being *within* the Catholic Church (in Latin: *in ipsa intus Catholica*), though his bond with the Church is not complete. In the next paragraph he continues:

> That the place of Baptism is sometimes supplied by suffering is supported by a substantial argument which the same Blessed Cyprian draws from the circumstance of the thief, to whom, although not baptized,[93] it was said: "Today thou shalt be with Me in paradise" (Lk. 23:43). Considering this again and again, I find that not only suffering for the name of Christ can make up for the lack of baptism, but also the Faith and conversion of heart, if it happens that lack of time prevents the celebration of the sacrament of baptism. For neither was that thief crucified for the name of Christ, but as the reward of his own deeds; nor did he suffer because he believed, but he believed while suffering. It was shown, therefore, in the case of that thief, how great is the power, even without the visible sacrament of baptism, of what the apostle says, "With the heart man believeth unto righteousness, and with the mouth confession is made unto salvation"(Rom. 10:10). But the want is supplied invisibly only when the administration of baptism is prevented, not by contempt for religion, but by the necessity of the moment.[94]

In the *City of God,* the same St. Augustine says:

> All those who, even without having received the laver of regeneration (Tit. 3:5), died for the profession of faith in Christ, (this passion) does for them as much to remit their sins, as if they were washed in the baptismal font. Indeed the same One who said: "Unless a man be born again of water and the Holy Ghost, he cannot enter into the kingdom of God" (Jn. 3:5), the same said in another sentence with no less generality: "Everyone therefore that shall confess me before men, I will also confess him before my Father who is in heaven" (Mt. 10:32) and in another place, "Whosoever will lose his life for my sake, shall find it"(Mt. 16:25). And this explains the verse, "Precious in the sight of the Lord is the death of His saints" (Ps. 115:15). For what is more

---

[93] In his *Retractations*, II, 44, St. Augustine says: "when I said that 'martyrdom could take place of baptism' I put an example that is not enough to the point, that of the thief, since it is unsure whether he was baptized or not"; as St. Bernard remarks in letter 77, §7, St. Augustine here corrects the example, but does not put in question the doctrine itself.

[94] *De Baptismo*, IV, 22, 29; R.J., No.1630, BAC, p.560.

precious than a death by which a man's sins are all forgiven, and his merits increased an hundredfold? For those who have been baptized when they could no longer escape death, and have departed this life with all their sins blotted out have not equal merit with those who did not defer death, though it was in their power to do so, but preferred to end their life by confessing Christ, rather than by denying Him to secure an opportunity of baptism. And even had they denied Him under pressure of the fear of death, this too would have been forgiven them in that baptism, in which was remitted even the enormous wickedness of those who had slain Christ. But how abundant in these men must have been the grace of the Spirit, who breathes where He wishes (Jn. 3:8), seeing that they so dearly loved Christ as to be unable to deny Him even in so sore an emergency, and with so sure a hope of pardon![95]

ST. GREGORY NAZIANZEN

§23: And so also in those who fail to receive the Gift [of Baptism], some are altogether animal or bestial, according as they are either foolish or wicked; and this, I think, has to be added to their other sins, that they have no reverence at all for this Gift, but look upon it as a mere gift—to be acquiesced in if given them, and if not given them, then to be neglected. Others know and honor the Gift, but put it off; some through laziness, some through greediness. Others are not in a position to receive it, perhaps on account of infancy, or some perfectly involuntary circumstance through which they are prevented from receiving it, even if they wish. As then in the former case we found much difference, so too in this. They who altogether despise it are worse than they who neglect it through greed or carelessness. These are worse than they who have lost the Gift through ignorance or tyranny, for tyranny is nothing but an involuntary error. And I think that the first will have to suffer punishment, as for all their sins, so for their contempt of baptism; and that the

---

[95] *De Civitate Dei*, 13:7; R.J., No.1759. Note that Fr. Feeney says exactly the contrary of St. Augustine: "Suppose a non-baptized person had his choice between Baptism of Water on the one hand, and what is called 'Baptism of Blood' on the other. Were he not to choose Baptism of Water, the shedding of his blood would be useless and he would lose his soul." (*Bread of Life*, p.41). Given the fact that the "choice" of baptism of blood is none other than either to deny Christ or to be killed, to affirm that one ought not to choose baptism of blood is to affirm that one should rather deny Christ. How impious!

second will also have to suffer, but less, because it was not so much through wickedness as through folly that they wrought their failure; and that the third will be neither glorified nor punished by the righteous Judge, as unsealed and yet not wicked, but persons who have suffered rather than done wrong. For not every one who is not bad enough to be punished is good enough to be honored; just as not every one who is not good enough to be honored is bad enough to be punished. And I look upon it as well from another point of view. If you judge the murderously disposed man by his will alone, apart from the act of murder, then you may reckon as baptized him who desired baptism apart from the reception of baptism. But if you cannot do the one how can you do the other? I cannot see it. Or, if you like, we will put it thus: If desire in your opinion has equal power with actual baptism, then judge in the same way in regard to glory, and you may be content with longing for it, as if that were itself glory. And what harm is done you by your not attaining the actual glory, as long as you have the desire for it?

§24: Therefore since you have heard these words, come forward to it, and be enlightened.[96]

The whole discourse is an exhortation to receive baptism. One must remember that, after the end of the persecutions, there were many converts; but, with less fervor than in previous times, some of these converts were falling into grievous sins and they found out that the Church was asking severe penances for these sins. So some thought it easier to wait as catechumens, and to be baptized later in life. St. Augustine is an example of this bad habit: he was a catechumen in his youth, but put it off and then fell into heresy (Manicheism), until the grace of God and the prayers and tears of his mother drew him back to the Church. Hence one finds in many Fathers of the fourth century such exhortations not to delay baptism. The first sentence of §24 has been put here precisely to show that such is the context of this sermon.

A superficial reading may lead one to think St. Gregory is against baptism of desire, but after reflection, one sees that, far from being against, he rather *sets the very principles of Baptism of Desire*. Indeed, the Church teaches that not any desire of baptism is sufficient for baptism of desire, but rather a firm resolution that only necessity prevents from execution. With this simple distinc-

---

[96] Discourse No.40, *On Baptism*.

tion in mind, let us consider of which desire St. Gregory speaks here.

Those who "are not in a position to receive it" are for instance those who, as infants, do not have the use of reason: in this case, St. Gregory exhorts those who are responsible for them not to delay their baptism. Notice that St. Gregory exposes here the principle of limbo: these will be "neither glorified nor punished by the righteous Judge." That only applies to those without the use of reason. (Some followers of Fr. Feeney would like us to think that infants in limbo suffer like in hell).

Others "are not in a position to receive it" but may have a "wish" for it, as in the case of "tyranny," *i.e.,* that they are under tyrannical authority preventing them from being baptized in spite of their wish. But what kind of wish is it? The key sentence is there: "If you judge the murderously disposed man by his will alone, apart from the act of murder, then you may reckon as baptized him who desired baptism apart from the reception of baptism." Now, if it were a firm will and resolution, such a sentence is only true of the human judge, but not of God: "for man seeth those things that appear, but the Lord beholdeth the heart" (I Kg 16:7); a human judge cannot condemn nor punish an interior sin nor reward an interior act of virtue, because he cannot see within the heart; hence the Church can never hold for certain that someone has baptism of desire.[97] But it is most sure that God, who sees the heart, does punish interior sins as the exterior: "But I say to you, that whosoever shall look on a woman to lust after her, hath already committed adultery with her in his heart" (Mt. 5:28). Given that murder is even worse than adultery, were St. Gregory speaking of such a real resolution and firm will, he could not say that "the murderously disposed man" would not be judged and condemned by God in case he is prevented from the exterior act of murder. Now, since God is more prompt to mercy than to punishment, and, as we have seen, He does punish sinful firm will and resolution even apart from the act, how much more does he reward righteous firm will and resolution even apart from the act,

---

[97] Baptism of blood is clearly exteriorly manifested, to give one's life for Christ and the true Faith is even the greatest profession of Faith! Hence the Church can canonize such persons, but never one with merely baptism of desire.

when the act is prevented with no fault from the person! One sees here the very principle of baptism of desire.

It is clear then, that St. Gregory speaks here of a mere wish and not a true will: and indeed, someone may feel an inclination to revenge and murder, but, fighting against it and not consenting to it, he has not a true will to murder, so he will not be condemned by God; similarly, someone who feels an inclination for baptism, but does not resolve firmly to be baptized and does not already conform his life to that of the faithful by a living faith, putting off one's baptism, such a one will not be rewarded by God.

The Authority of Doctors

St. Bernard

He has a whole letter (No. 77) on Baptism to Hugh of St. Victor, a famous theologian of his time, in which he treats *ex professo* this question in §6-8. Hugh had asked St. Bernard for his views on several novelties of an unnamed person, one of these being the denial of baptism of desire. We give this passage in full, so that the reader may have a taste of the way the holy Doctors argue in defense of the traditional doctrine.

> §6. If an adult...wish and seek to be baptized, but is unable to obtain it because death intervenes, then where there is no lack of right faith, devout hope, sincere charity, may God be gracious to me, because I cannot completely despair of salvation for such a one solely on account of water, if it be lacking, and cannot believe that faith will be rendered empty, hope confounded and charity lost, provided only that he is not contemptuous of the water, but as I said merely kept from it by lack of opportunity...
>
> §7. But I am very much astonished if this new inventor of new assertions and assertor of inventions has been able to find in this matter arguments which escaped the notice of the holy fathers Ambrose and Augustine or an authority greater than their authority. [He then quotes both passages given above...]
>
> §8. Believe me, it will be difficult to separate me from these two columns, by which I refer to Augustine and Ambrose...believing with them that people can be saved by faith alone and the desire to receive the sacrament, however only in the case that un-

timely death or some other insuperable force keep them from fulfilling their pious desire.

Notice also that, when the Savior said "whoever believes and is baptized will be saved," He cautiously and alertly did not repeat the phrase "who was not baptized," but only "whoever does not believe will be condemned" (Mk. 16:16). This intimated that sometimes faith alone would suffice for salvation, and that without it, nothing would be sufficient.

For this reason, even if it is granted that martyrdom can take the place of baptism, it is clearly not the penalty which does this, but faith itself. For without faith what is martyrdom, if not a penalty? It is faith's doing that martyrdom can without any doubt be considered the equivalent of baptism. Would not faith be very sickly and weak in itself, if what it can give to another, it cannot obtain by itself? To be sure, to pour out one's blood for Christ is an indubitable proof of great faith–but to men, not to God. But what if God, who needs to perform no experiments to test for what He wants, saw great faith in the heart of someone dying in peace, not put to the question by martyrdom, but suitable for martyrdom nevertheless? If he remembers that he has not yet received the sacrament and sorrowfully and repentantly asks for it with all his heart, but cannot receive it because his death comes too quickly, will God damn his faithful one? Will He damn, I ask, a person who is even prepared to die for Him? Paul says: "No one can say Jesus is Lord, except in the Holy Ghost" (I Cor. 12:3). Will we say that such a one, who at the moment of death not only invokes the Lord Jesus, but asks for the sacrament with his every longing, either does not speak in the Holy Ghost, so that the Apostle was mistaken, or is damned even though he has the Holy Ghost? He has the Savior dwelling in his heart by faith (Eph 3:17) and in his mouth by confession (Rom 10:10); will he then be damned with the Savior? Certainly if martyrdom obtains its prerogative only by the merit of faith, so that it is safely and singularly accepted in the place of baptism, I do not see why faith itself cannot with equal cause and without martyrdom be just as great in God's eyes, who knows of it without the proof of martyrdom. I would say it can be just as great as far as obtaining salvation goes, but it is not as great in regard to the accumulation of merit, in which martyrdom surely surpasses it.

We read: "Everyone who hates his brother is a murderer" (I Jn. 3:15); and again, "Whoever looks at a woman lustfully has already committed adultery with her in his heart" (Mt. 5:28).

How could it be more evident that the wish is considered the equivalent of the deed, when necessity excludes the deed? That is, unless one thinks that God, who is love, would impute us the evil deeds of the will and not the good, and that the merciful and compassionate Lord is more ready to punish than to reward.

Suppose someone who is at the point of death happens to remember that he is bound by a debt to another. If he lacks the means to pay it, he is still believed to obtain pardon solely by repentance and contrition of heart, and so he is not damned on account of it. In the same way, faith alone and turning the mind to God, without the spilling of blood or the pouring of water, doubtlessly bring salvation to one who has the will but not the way—because death intervenes—to be baptized. And just as in the former case no repentance remits sin if, when he can, he does not restore what he owes, so in the latter faith is of no avail, if, when he can, he does not receive the sacrament. He is shown not to have perfect faith, if he neglects to do so. True and full faith complies with all the commandments; this particular commandment is the foremost of them all. Rightly, then, anyone who refuses to obey will be thought of not as faithful, but as rebellious and disdainful. How can someone be faithful, if he holds a sacrament of God in contempt?

St. Albert the Great

Opera Omnia, Vol. XXVI, pp.35-40: Tract. III, *De Baptismo* Q.I, art.7.

St. Bonaventure

Commentaria in Lib. Sententiarum IV, dist.4, p.2, Art.1, Quest.1.

St. Thomas Aquinas

In his *Summa Theologica*, St. Thomas Aquinas[98] gave, in a very clear way, the doctrine of the Church, seven hundred years ago! We give here the full text of the three questions dealing explicitly with Baptism of Desire; the reader will admire the conciseness and depth of St. Thomas's teaching, which makes of the

---

[98] In three articles of the *Summa Theologica*, III, Q.66, A.11-12 and Q.68, A.2.

Summa such a delight. As we have seen above,[99] St. Thomas mentions baptism of desire in other places of his works, but it is of course impossible to give every quote!

One word to help the reader who is not acquainted with the theology of the sacraments. St. Thomas distinguishes three elements in each sacrament: *1) sacramentum tantum*–the exterior sign (*e.g.*, water in baptism); *2) sacramentum et res*–a "sign and reality," (*e.g.*, the character of baptism) an intermediary element, signified and effected by the exterior sign, but itself further signifying and causing the ultimate reality, grace; *3) res tantum*–the reality itself, *i.e.*, the ultimate reality signified in the sacrament, that is the *sacramental grace*, *i.e.*, sanctifying grace with a special fruitfulness to further actual graces to practice the virtues proper to each sacrament (graces to live as a child of God, as a soldier of Christ, as a priest of Christ, as a good Christian spouse, *etc.*). Baptism of blood and baptism of desire are called "baptism" because they produce the *reality itself* of the sacrament of baptism, *i.e.*, they wash sin and give sanctifying grace, the life of the soul, the new birth.

Whether three kinds of baptism are fittingly described, that is, baptism of water, of blood, and of the Spirit? (*Summa Theologica*, III, Q.66, A.11.)

Obj. 1: It seems that the three kinds of Baptism are not fittingly described as Baptism of Water, of Blood, and of the Spirit, *i.e.*, of the Holy Ghost. Because the Apostle says (Eph. 4:5): "One Faith, one Baptism." Now there is but one Faith. Therefore there should not be three Baptisms.

Obj. 2: Further, Baptism is a sacrament, as we have made clear above (Q.65, A.1). Now none but Baptism of Water is a sacrament. Therefore we should not reckon two other Baptisms.

Obj. 3: Further, Damascene (*De Fide Orth.*, iv) distinguishes several other kinds of Baptism. Therefore we should admit more than three Baptisms.

On the contrary, on Heb. 6:2, "Of the doctrine of Baptisms," the gloss says: "He uses the plural, because there is Baptism of Water, of Repentance, and of Blood."

---

[99] *ST*, III, Q.68, A.3, see p.47; *ST*, Q.73, A.3, see p.38.

I answer that, as stated above (Q.62, A.5) baptism of water has its efficacy from Christ's Passion, to which a man is conformed by baptism, and also from the Holy Ghost. Now although the effect depends on the first cause, the cause far surpasses the effect, nor does it depend on it. Consequently, a man may, without baptism of water, receive the sacramental effect from Christ's Passion, in so far as he is conformed to Christ by suffering for Him. Hence it is written (Apoc. 7:14) "These are they who are come out of great tribulation, and have washed their robes and have made them white in the blood of the Lamb." In like manner a man receives the effect of baptism by the power of the Holy Ghost, not only without baptism of water, but also without baptism of blood; forasmuch as his heart is moved by the Holy Ghost to believe in and love God and to repent of his sins; wherefore this is also called baptism of repentance. Of this it is written (Is. 4:4): "If the Lord shall wash away the filth of the daughters of Zion, and shall wash away the blood of Jerusalem out of the midst thereof, by the spirit of judgment, and by the spirit of burning." Thus, therefore, each of these other Baptisms is called baptism, forasmuch as it takes the place of baptism. Wherefore Augustine says ("Of the Unique Baptism of Infants," IV): "The Blessed Cyprian argues with considerable reason from the thief to whom, though not baptized, it was said: 'Today shalt thou be with me in Paradise' that suffering can take the place of baptism. Having weighed this in my mind again and again, I perceive that not only can suffering for the name of Christ supply for what was lacking in baptism, but even faith and conversion of heart, if perchance on account of the stress of the times the celebration of the mystery of baptism is not practicable."

Ad 1: The other two Baptisms are included in the Baptism of Water,[100] which derives its efficacy, both from Christ's Passion and from the Holy Ghost. Consequently for this reason the unity of Baptism is not destroyed.

Ad 2: As stated above (Q.60, A.1), a sacrament is a kind of sign. The other two, however, are like the Baptism of Water,

---

[100] St. Thomas argues from the unity of the first cause and ultimate reality of baptism: there is ONE new birth, one washing of the soul, effected by each of these three baptism. Baptism is a Greek word signifying washing: the main washing is that of the soul, signified by the exterior washing by water. Since there is one interior washing, the two other means of it "are included" in the main one.

not, indeed, in the nature of sign, but in the baptismal effect. Consequently they are not sacraments.

Ad 3: Damascene enumerates certain figurative Baptisms. For instance, "the Deluge" was a figure of our Baptism, in respect of the salvation of the faithful in the Church; since then "a few...souls were saved in the ark [Vulg.: 'by water']," according to I Pt. 3:20. He also mentions "the crossing of the Red Sea": which was a figure of our Baptism, in respect of our delivery from the bondage of sin; hence the Apostle says (I Cor. 10:2) that "all...were baptized in the cloud and in the sea." And again he mentions "the various washings which were customary under the Old Law," which were figures of our Baptism, as to the cleansing from sins: also "the Baptism of John," which prepared the way for our Baptism.

Whether the Baptism of Blood is the most excellent of these? (*Summa Theologica*, III, Q.66, A.12)

Obj. 1: It seems that the Baptism of Blood is not the most excellent of these three. For the Baptism of Water impresses a character; which the Baptism of Blood cannot do. Therefore the Baptism of Blood is not more excellent than the Baptism of Water.

Obj. 2: Further, the Baptism of Blood is of no avail without the Baptism of the Spirit, which is by charity; for it is written (I Cor. 13:3): "If I should deliver my body to be burned, and have not charity, it profiteth me nothing." But the Baptism of the Spirit avails without the Baptism of Blood; for not only the martyrs are saved. Therefore the Baptism of Blood is not the most excellent.

Obj. 3: Further, just as the Baptism of Water derives its efficacy from Christ's Passion, to which, as stated above (A.11), the Baptism of Blood corresponds, so Christ's Passion derives its efficacy from the Holy Ghost, according to Heb. 9:14: "The Blood of Christ, Who by the Holy Ghost offered Himself unspotted unto God, shall cleanse our conscience from dead works," *etc.* Therefore the Baptism of the Spirit is more excellent than the Baptism of Blood. Therefore the Baptism of Blood is not the most excellent.

On the contrary, Augustine (*Ad Fortunatum*) speaking of the comparison between Baptisms says: "The newly baptized confesses his faith in the presence of the priest; the martyr in the presence of the persecutor. The former is sprinkled with water, after he has confessed; the latter with his blood. The former receives the Holy Ghost by the imposition of the bishop's hands; the latter is made the temple of the Holy Ghost."

I answer that, the shedding of blood for Christ's sake, and the inward operation of the Holy Ghost, are called baptisms, in so far as they produce the effect of the baptism of water. Now the baptism of water derives its efficacy from Christ's Passion and from the Holy Ghost, as already stated (*ibid.*). These two causes act in each of these three baptisms; most excellently, however, in the baptism of blood. For Christ's Passion acts in the baptism of water by way of a figurative representation; in the baptism of the spirit of repentance, by way of desire; but in the baptism of blood, by way of imitating the act itself. In like manner, too, the power of the Holy Ghost acts in the baptism of water through a certain hidden power; in the baptism of repentance by moving the heart; but in the baptism of blood by the highest degree of fervor of dilection and love, according to John (15:13): "Greater love than this no man hath that a man lay down his life for his friends."

Ad 1: A character is both reality and a sacrament. And we do not say that the Baptism of Blood is more excellent, considering the nature of a sacrament; but considering the sacramental effect.[101]

Ad 2: The shedding of blood is not in the nature of a baptism if it be without charity. Hence it is clear that the Baptism of Blood includes the Baptism of the Spirit, but not conversely. And from this it is proved to be more perfect.

Ad 3: The Baptism owes its pre-eminence not only to Christ's Passion, but also to the Holy Ghost, as stated above.

Whether a man can be saved without baptism? (*Summa Theologica*, III, Q.68, A.2)

Obj. 1: It seems that no man can be saved without Baptism. For our Lord said (Jn. 3:5): "Unless a man be born again of water and the Holy Ghost, he cannot enter the kingdom of God." But those alone are saved who enter God's kingdom. Therefore none can be saved without Baptism, by which a man is born again of water and the Holy Ghost.

---

[101] In other words, it is not a *better sign*, but gives a better ultimate effect, *a greater grace and salvation.*

Obj. 2: Further, in the book *De Eccl. Dogm.* xli, it is written: "We believe that no catechumen, though he die in his good works, will have eternal life, except he suffer martyrdom, which contains all the sacramental virtue of Baptism." But if it were possible for anyone to be saved without Baptism, this would be the case specially with catechumens who are credited with good works, for they seem to have the "faith that worketh by charity" (Gal. 5:6). Therefore it seems that none can be saved without Baptism.

Obj. 3: Further, as stated above (A.1; Q.65, A.4), the sacrament of Baptism is necessary for salvation. Now that is necessary "without which something cannot be" (*Metaph.* v). Therefore it seems that none can obtain salvation without Baptism.

On the contrary, Augustine says (*Super Levit.* lxxxiv) that "some have received the invisible sanctification without visible sacraments, and to their profit; but though it is possible to have the visible sanctification, consisting in a visible sacrament, without the invisible sanctification, it will be to no profit." Since, therefore, the sacrament of Baptism pertains to the visible sanctification, it seems that a man can obtain salvation without the sacrament of Baptism, by means of the invisible sanctification.

I answer that, the sacrament of baptism may be wanting to someone in two ways. First, both in reality and in desire; as is the case with those who neither are baptized, nor wished to be baptized; which clearly indicates contempt of the sacrament, in regard to those who have the use of the free-will. Consequently those to whom baptism is wanting thus, cannot obtain salvation; since neither sacramentally nor mentally are they incorporated in Christ,[102] through whom alone can salvation be obtained.

Secondly, the sacrament of baptism may be wanting to anyone in reality but not in desire; for instance, when a man wishes to be baptized, but by some ill-chance he is forestalled by death before receiving baptism. And such a man can obtain salvation without being actually baptized, on account of his desire for baptism, which desire is the outcome of faith that worketh by charity, whereby God, Whose power is not tied to visible sacraments, sanctifies man inwardly. Hence Ambrose says of Valentinian, who died while yet a catechumen: "I lost him whom I was to regenerate, but he did not lose the grace he prayed for."

---

[102] It is clear from this that, according to St. Thomas, baptism of desire does *incorporate in Christ*, hence makes someone member of the Mystical Body of Christ, the Church, though the bond is spiritual and not yet complete.

Ad 1: As it is written (I Kgs. 16:7), "man seeth those things that appear, but the Lord beholdeth the heart." Now a man who desires to be "born again of water and the Holy Ghost" by Baptism, is regenerated in heart though not in body. Thus the Apostle says (Rm. 2:29) that "the circumcision is that of the heart, in the spirit, not in the letter; whose praise is not of men but of God."

Ad 2: No man obtains eternal life unless he be free from all guilt and debt of punishment. Now this plenary absolution is given when a man receives Baptism, or suffers martyrdom: for which reason is it stated that martyrdom "contains all the sacramental virtue of Baptism," *i.e.*, as to the full deliverance from guilt and punishment. Suppose, therefore, a catechumen to have the desire for Baptism (else he could not be said to die in his good works, which cannot be without "faith that worketh by charity"), such a one, were he to die, would not forthwith come to eternal life, but would suffer punishment for his past sins [in Purgatory], "but he himself shall be saved, yet so as by fire" as is stated in I Cor. 3:15.

Ad 3: The sacrament of Baptism is said to be necessary for salvation in so far as man cannot be saved without, at least, Baptism of desire; "which, with God, counts for the deed" (Augustine, *Enarr. in Ps. 57*).[103]

Thus the Church has not changed its doctrine one iota from that of St. Thomas, which is clearly based on the Scriptures and the Fathers of the Church.

ST. ROBERT BELLARMINE

Though their teaching encompasses often the whole of Catholic doctrine, each Doctor of the Church has somehow his "specialty," for instance, St. Alphonsus is renowned for moral theology, St. Augustine for grace, St. Bernard for Our Lady, *etc.* St. Robert is renowned for his treatise on the Church. So his teaching on the question merits particular attention. In his masterpiece on the Church, he defines the Church thus:

> Our definition is: there is only one Church, not two, and this one and true Church is the congregation of men bound together

---

[103] St. Thomas here explains *what kind of necessity* is that of the exterior sacrament: a necessity *re aut voto–in fact or in desire*, as will be defined later by the Council of Trent in general for all sacraments.

by the profession of the same Christian faith, and the communion to the same sacraments, under the government of the legitimate shepherds, and chiefly of the one vicar of Christ on earth, the Roman Pontiff. There are thus three parts to this definition: the profession of the true faith, the sacramental communion and the submission to the legitimate shepherd, the Roman Pontiff.[104]

This definition can be found in equivalent terms in Pope Pius XII's encyclical on the Church *Mystici Corporis*. St. Robert considers the difficulty:

> Concerning catechumens there is a greater difficulty, because they are faithful [have the faith] and can be saved if they die in this state, and yet outside the Church no one is saved, as outside the ark of Noah...

He then gives answers which he judges inadequate, such as that of Melchior Cano, then he gives his answer:

> I answer therefore that, when it is said *outside the Church no one is saved*, it must be understood of those who belong to her neither in actual fact nor in desire [*desiderio*], as theologians commonly speak on baptism. Because the catechumens are in the Church, though not in actual fact, yet at least in resolution [*voto*], therefore they can be saved.[105]

It is not without interest to note what he writes about the lack of the third bond, ecclesiastical communion:

> It may happen that an excommunicated man retains his baptism, the profession of faith and the subjection to the legitimate prelates, and thus be a friend of God, if his excommunication was unjust; it may also happen that a man justly excommunicated does penance, and have the above three before he receives the absolution, and thus he would be in the Church, even while remaining still excommunicated. I answer that such *a man is in the Church by his soul, i.e., by desire, which is sufficient for him unto salvation*, but he is not yet by his body, *i.e.*, by external communion, which makes one properly speaking member of the visible Church on earth.[106]

Then St. Bellarmine quotes St. Augustine, *De Vera Religione*, Ch.6, No.11. [See note No.158].

---

[104] *De Ecclesia Militante,* Book III, Ch.2, *opera omnia*, Naples 1872, p.75.
[105] *Ibid.* Ch.3, "Of those who are not baptized," p.76.
[106] *Ibid.* Ch.6, "Of the excommunicated."

Also he wrote *De Sacramento Baptismi*, Liber I, Chapter VI: the whole chapter is on baptism of blood and baptism of desire. He interestingly exposes at length the common teaching that baptism of blood applies also to infants (*e.g.*, who are martyred with their parents). He quotes in this chapter in favor of baptism of blood and desire, apart from those Fathers above mentioned, St. Jerome and St. John Damascene, who affirm the existence of these baptisms: these Fathers do not say that these baptisms supply for the lack of water, but St. Albert the Great in the above mentioned passage, which St. Robert quotes, explains that they would not deserve the name of baptism if they had not the power to give the first justification

St. Alphonsus Liguori

> Baptism of desire is perfect conversion to God which, through contrition or love of God above all things along with the explicit or implicit desire of true Baptism of water; it supplies its power, according to Trent, with regard to the remission of the fault, but not the impression of the character, nor with regard to the complete taking away of the punishment due sin–thus teach Viva, the Salmanticenses, along with Suarez, Vasquez, Valentia; Croix and others [he gives the references]. *It is* **de fide** *that men can be saved through baptism of desire*: according to *Apostolicam*,[107] concerning a priest not baptized; and according to Trent (Session 6, On Justification, Chapter 4), where it is said that no man can be saved "without the laver of regeneration or its desire."[108] [The next three paragraphs are on baptism of blood.]

Note that St. Alphonsus, knowing that the Council of Trent teaches that the justified has all that is necessary for salvation, draws the conclusion: it is *de fide* that men can be *saved* through baptism of desire.

---

[107] Name of the constitution of Innocent III, see above p.43, Dz. 388
[108] *Theologia Moralis*, Lib.6, Tr.2, Cap.1, No.96.

The Authority of Other Saints or Theologians

CATECHISM OF THE COUNCIL OF TRENT

It is the obligatory model of Catechisms: "On adults, however, the Church...has ordained that [Baptism] be deferred for a certain time. The delay is not attended with the same danger as in the case of infants...should any unforeseen accident make it impossible for adults to be washed in the salutary waters, their intention and determination to receive Baptism and their repentance for past sins, will avail them to grace and righteousness"[109] (and thus salvation, since it is explicitly a question of danger of death, see the previous page).

HOLY MYSTICS

St. Catherine of Siena speaks of these three baptisms in her dialogue, in a vision which she received from Christ, explaining the water (baptism of water) and blood (baptism of blood) coming out of the side of Christ (baptism of the fire of charity).[110]

St. John Bosco in his dream on April 3, 1861, saw three lakes of blood, water and fire, and explained that they were the three paths to heaven, the *Three Baptisms*.[111]

THEOLOGIANS

Hugh of St. Victor, *De Sacramentis*, II, 6, 7; also *Summa Sententiarum*, Tract. V, Caput 5 and Cap. 7. He writes at the end of Chapter 5:

> Some say that it is impossible that anyone should have faith and charity and yet die without baptism, for, as they say, God would not permit them to die without baptism. But, it seems to me, that since they are not counselors of God, it is foolish and presumptuous [*stultum et temerarium*] for them to affirm this.

The following theologians were standard textbooks in seminaries, all approved by the authorities of the Church. Their value

---

[109] *Catechism of the Council of Trent*, published by TAN, p.179.
[110] *The Dialogue of Saint Catherine of Siena*, (Rockford, IL: TAN Books and Publishers, 1974), pp.170-175.
[111] *The Dreams of St. John Bosco*, Salesian Press in Taiwan, 1982.

is in their total agreement on the matter. There is not a single one disagreeing. In *Mancipia*, Saint Benedict Center's newsletter, July 1998, the followers of Fr. Feeney themselves acknowledge: "This teaching indeed was and is the common teaching of theologians since the early part of this millennium" (second millennium). It is not only the *common* teaching, but *unanimous* teaching; it is not only since the early part of this millennium, but rather from the beginning of the Church as the section on the Fathers has clearly shown.

Cardinal Billot, S.J., *De Ecclesia Christi,* Qu.7, Th.14 (1909); *De Ecclesiae Sacramentis* Th.24, Th.25 (Roma 1924) pp.240-261; *De Gratia Christi,* Th.13, p.197*sqq*. He has this good explanation: "Baptism of blood and of the Spirit, because they do not impress the character, do not fully insert a man in the Church. However, the martyrs are already publicly, really and juridically of the Church, though of themselves they are not yet apt to receive the other sacraments. By Baptism of the Spirit is already an *ordination to the body of the Church,*[112] juridical for the public catechumens, but not complete, according to St. Augustine: 'you are *not yet reborn* by the sacred baptism, but you are *already conceived* in the bosom of our Holy Mother the Church.'"

Cornelius a Lapide writes on his commentary of Mt. 3:11:

> Hence the Doctors assign a triple baptism, of water, of the Spirit and of blood. Baptism of water is when one is washed with water. Baptism of the Spirit is when a catechumen in prison or in the desert where there is no water, is truly contrite for his sins, and wants to be baptized: such a one is justified by contrition which includes the desire for baptism. Baptism of Blood is when someone not yet baptized, dies as martyr for the faith: such a one is baptized in his own blood and cleansed from all his sins.[113]

Franzelin, *De Ecclesia* (Rome, 1987), pp.414-423. His article is particularly interesting because he shows that the catechumens

---

[112] Knowing how carefully Pope Pius XII used to prepare his encyclicals, it seems to me that perhaps here is the source from which he took this expression for his encyclical *Mystici Corporis.*

[113] Cornelius a Lapide, *Commentaria in Sacram Scripturam,* (Naples, 1857), Vol.8, p.74.

are not foreign to the Church: he gives a quote of Eusebius and a reference to Origen counting them as the lowest "order of the Church," and a quote of St. Augustine counting them as "already belonging to the great House [of God]," but not yet as sons. He shows that they are already subject to the teaching authority of the Church, and to some of the discipline of the Church who has established special laws for the catechumens. Then he states the traditional teaching on Baptism of Blood and Baptism of Desire. He concludes:

> What the Apostle says of the members of the Church: 'one body, one Spirit...in one hope of your vocation, one Lord, one faith, one baptism' (Eph. 4:4), that is ***totally found*** in these justified [catechumens] as far as that which is spiritual: they have the one Spirit, and thus the one charity in one faith and one hope of the vocation, and therefore they adhere to the one Lord (see I Cor. 6:17); however, the visible elements which the Apostle sets together with the invisible ones, and which must be bound with them from the very institution and law of Christ, is found in them not in act but only in the resolve of the will: 'one body and one baptism.' Thus, since according to the teaching of the Apostle 'we are baptized in one body,' those [justified catechumens] who lack baptism, these **belong to the *one body*** not *simpliciter* [absolutely] but *secundum quid* [according to some reason], yet by charity and the very resolve of the will they are in the one Spirit.

Garrigou-Lagrange, *De Revelatione,* (Rome, 1925), pp.613-615. He uses the expressions *body* of the Church, *soul* of the Church. One must see the reality meant by these words and not the words themselves. This vocabulary was commonly used before Pius XII. This Pope rightly corrected this vocabulary, and thus we must translate Garrigou's position with better wording (but the *meaning* remains the same!) Garrigou sums up his thesis as: "It is necessary, of a necessity of means, to belong really to the soul of the Church; [it is necessary] for adults to belong to the body of the Church *in re aut in voto* (or implicit desire), for children *in re*." In other words, he teaches the necessity to have in reality the spiritual bond with the Church, which is sanctifying grace with true Faith, Hope and Charity; it is necessary for adults to have *re aut voto* (at least the implicit desire) the exterior bond with the Church, which is the profession of Faith, union of worship (starting with the reception of Baptism), and submission to the Sovereign Pontiff; for children (before the use of reason), it is necessary to have *in re* the exterior bond by the reception of Baptism (which is the first profession of faith and virtually includes submission to the Sovereign Pontiff).

We shall give now three more testimonies, by Bishop George Hay, Fr. Michael Müller, C.Ss.R., and Orestes Brownson. These three Catholic authors are often quoted by followers of Fr. Feeney, and presented as the best champions of the dogma *outside the Church there is no salvation*. But they too hold to the doctrine of Baptism of Blood and Baptism of Desire! Ought not the followers of Fr. Feeney to follow the very champions they propose? They cannot give a single author who clearly rejects this Catholic teaching!

BISHOP GEORGE HAY

> Though Jesus Christ expressly says, "Except a man be born again of water and the Holy Spirit, he cannot enter into the kingdom of God" (Jn. 3:5), which establishes the absolute necessity of baptism for salvation; yet, suppose a heathen, or a Turk, or Jew, should be instructed in the faith of Christ, and embrace it with all his heart, but die suddenly without baptism, or be taken away by his infidel friends, or put in absolute impossibility of receiving baptism, and die in the above dispositions with a sincere repentance and desire of baptism, this person will undoubtedly receive all the fruits of baptism from God; and therefore, is said to be baptized in desire. In the same manner, suppose a person brought up in a false religion, embraces with all his heart the light of the true faith, which God gives him in his last moments, as it is absolutely impossible for him, in that state, to join the external communion of the Church in the eyes of men, yet he will surely be considered as united to her in the sight of God, by means of the true faith which he embraces, and his desire of being united to the Church, if it were in his power.[114]

FR. MICHAEL MÜLLER, C.SS.R.

> Q.8. Can the baptism of water be ever supplied?

---

[114] See the examples, p.84. *The Sincere Christian* (Blackwood, 1873), II, 599, 600.

When a person cannot receive the baptism of water, it may be supplied by the baptism of desire or by the baptism of blood.

Almighty God is goodness itself. Hence he wishes that all men should be saved. But in order to be saved, it is necessary to pass, by means of baptism, from the state of sin to the state of grace. Infants, therefore, who die unbaptized, can never enter the kingdom of heaven. The case of grown persons is somewhat different; for, when grown persons cannot be actually baptized before death, then the baptism of water may be supplied by what is called *baptism of desire*.

There is an infidel. He has become acquainted with the true faith. He most earnestly desires baptism. But he cannot have any one to baptize him before he dies. Now, is such a person lost because he dies without the baptism of water? No; in this case, the person is said to be baptized *in desire*.

Q.9. What is the baptism of desire?

An earnest wish to receive baptism, or to do all that God requires of us for our salvation, together with a perfect contrition, or a perfect love of God.

An ardent desire of baptism, accompanied with faith in Jesus Christ and true repentance, is, with God, like the baptism of water. In this case, the words of the Blessed Virgin are verified: "The Lord has filled the hungry with good things" (Lk. 1:35). He bestows the good things of heaven upon those who die with the desire of baptism [...]

Although it be true that the fathers of the Church have believed and taught that the baptism of desire may supply the baptism of water, yet this doctrine, as St. Augustine observes, should not make any one delay ordinary baptism when he is able to receive it; for, such a delay of baptism is always attended with great danger [to] salvation.

Q.10. What is the baptism of blood?

Martyrdom for the sake of Christ.

There is still another case in which a person may be justified and saved without having actually received the sacrament of baptism, *viz.*: the case of a person suffering martyrdom for the faith before he has been able to receive baptism. Martyrdom for the true faith has always been held by the Church to supply the sacrament of baptism. Hence, in the case of martyrdom, a person has always been said to be baptized in his own blood. Our divine

Savior assures us that "whosoever shall lose his life for [My] sake and the gospel, shall save it" (Mk. 8:35). He, therefore, who dies for Jesus Christ, and for the sake of his religion, obtains a full remission of all his sins, and is immediately after death admitted into heaven.[115]

ORESTES BROWNSON

It is evident, both from Bellarmine and Billuart, that no one can be saved unless he belongs to the visible communion of the Church, either actually or virtually, and also that the salvation of catechumens can be asserted only because they do so belong; that is, because they are in the vestibule, for the purpose of entering,– have already entered in their will and proximate disposition. St. Thomas teaches with regard to these, in case they have faith working by love, that all they lack is the reception of the visible sacrament *in re*; but if they are prevented by death from receiving it *in re* before the Church is ready to administer it, that God supplies the defect, accepts the will for the deed, and reputes them to be baptized. If the defect is supplied, and God reputes them to be baptized, they are so in effect, have in effect received the visible sacrament,[116] are truly members of the external communion of the Church, and therefore are saved in it, not out of if.

Bellarmine, Billuart, Perrone, *etc.*, in speaking of persons as belonging to the soul and not to the body, mean, it is evident, not persons who in no sense belong to the body, but simply those who, though they in effect belong to it, do not belong to it in the full and strict sense of the word, because they have not received the visible sacrament *in re*. All they teach is simply that persons may be saved who have not received the visible sacrament *in re*; but they by no means teach that persons can be saved without having received the visible sacrament at all. There is no difference between their view and ours, for we have never contended for anything more than this; only we think, that, in these times especially, when the tendency is to depreciate the external, it is more proper to speak of them simply as belonging to the soul, for the fact the most important to be insisted on is, not that it is impossible to be saved without receiving the visible sacra-

---

[115] *God the Teacher of Mankind: Grace and the Sacraments,* (Benzinger, 1877), pp.218-222.
[116] That is, have received the effect of the visible sacrament, not the exterior visible sign itself.

ment *in re*, but that it is impossible to be saved without receiving the visible sacrament at least *in voto et proxima dispositione*.[117]

Further references can be found in the bibliography in Appendix I.

TWO TYPICAL EXAMPLES OF BAPTISM OF DESIRE

There was in the 19th century in France a very famous converted Jew, Fr. Augustine Marie of the Blessed Sacrament, born Hermann Cohen. After his conversion, he became a Carmelite monk and a renowned preacher. He restored the Carmelite Order in England.

He worked hard for the conversion of his family. By the grace of God, he succeeded in the conversion of his sister and her son; but he did not succeed with the conversion of his mother. He prayed, made sacrifices, talked with her, to no avail. She died with no apparent sign of repentance. The poor monk was so sad, yet never despaired in the mercy of the Sacred Heart.

For several years, God left him in this trial; but one day he met the holy Curé of Ars, who told him: "Hope, hope, you shall receive one day, on the Feast of the Immaculate Conception, a letter that shall bring you great consolation."

Indeed, on the Feast of the Immaculate Conception 1861, he received a letter from a pious soul, Léonie Guillemant, saying:

> My Jesus gave me a beam of His Divine Light…At the moment when Fr. Hermann's mother was almost giving her last breath, when she looked unconscious, almost without life, Mary, our good Mother, came in front of her Divine Son and, falling on her knees at His feet, she said to Him: "Grace, Mercy, O my Son, for this perishing soul. In a few moments, she shall be lost, lost for ever. I beseech Thee, do for the mother of my servant Hermann what Thou wouldst him to do for Thine, if she would be in her place and Thee at his place. The soul of his mother is his dearest good, a thousand times he dedicated it to me; he entrusted it to the tenderness and solicitude of my Heart. Could I bear to see it perish? No, no, this soul is mine, I want it, I claim it as my inheritance, bought at the price of Thy Blood, of my Sorrows at the foot of Thy Cross!"

---

[117] *They Have Fought the Good Fight*, "The Great Question," pp.131, 132.

As soon as she ended this divine supplication, a strong and powerful grace came forth from the source of all graces, the adorable Heart of our Jesus, and enlightened the soul of the poor dying Jewess and triumphed instantaneously over her resistances. This soul turned around with love and confidence towards Him whose mercy followed her even in the arms of death and she said (in her heart): "O Jesus, God of the Christians, God that my son adores, I believe, I hope in Thee, have mercy on me!"

The pious soul who had this vision was a complete stranger to Fr. Hermann; the fact of her vision is not only known by the letter she wrote to Fr. Hermann, but also in her own family by her nephew Emile Baumann; it is greatly authenticated by the prophecy of the holy Curé of Ars.[118]

The second example is that of the "Canutes," a tribe near Chartres in France. When the first missionaries arrived there, they found druids who worshipped "the Virgin who shall conceive." They told them, "We know that Virgin, she is called Mary; we preach to you her Son, Jesus Christ, the Savior of the world!" And the whole tribe was converted. It was not exactly a "conversion" but rather a fulfillment of their already existing faith in the "Son of the Virgin." What must have happened, is that a pious soul had received a revelation from an angel that "The Virgin shall conceive, and she shall bring forth a child. He is the Savior of the world!" They had not yet baptism, but by believing in the "Son of the Virgin" and living worthily of Him, they could be saved.[119]

Conclusion: *eodem Sensu, eademque Sententia*

Dear reader, arrived at this point, when we consider together all this concordant teaching of the Church, we can have but one faithful attitude, that of receiving this teaching, holding fast to it *in eodem sensu, eademque sententia*–in the same sense and the same words (I Cor. 1:10). The doctrine of baptism of blood and baptism of desire is inseparably linked by the Church to the dogma *outside the Church there is no salvation*. It belongs to the very proper understanding of that dogma, so much that if one denies it, he

---

[118] *Flèche de Feu*, pp.259, 260.
[119] Very short reference to this is made in *Chartres Cathedral*, by Malcolm Miller.

no longer holds the dogma *in the same sense and the same words* as the Church holds it.

Did not Fr. Feeney know all of these texts? Yes he did; according to Bro. Michael, Fr. Feeney, was well aware of them, but he "found it necessary to improve (*sic*) upon the teaching of some of the Doctors."[120] This seems quite presumptuous. So much the more that to negate what the Fathers and Doctors positively taught is not an improvement, but rather an infidelity to their teaching. No! Instead of all these efforts to minimize or revise this teaching of the Fathers, Doctors and popes, one should rather humbly "hold fast to the doctrine of the Fathers,"[121] Doctors and popes!

Why did Bro. Michael write that St. Thomas's teaching in the *Summa* on baptism of desire "is merely his own theological speculation"[122] if he is "very much aware of"[123] all the quotes of the Fathers?

It seems that some followers of Fr. Feeney were not aware of all these texts. For instance, one wrote: "the so-called baptisms of desire and blood are liberal inventions."[124] Being a point of doctrine on exceptional situations, one may have an *invincible ignorance* on it. However, after reading the documentation above, it is impossible to hold such a position any longer.

Faced with all these texts, they try three escapes.

First, they attack the authority of the Doctors. Bro. Robert writes: "Aquinas was a saint and a brilliant theologian, but he was not infallible! Just as his opinion in the two instances cited were wrong [Immaculate Conception and animation in the womb], his opinions concerning the efficacy of 'desire' could well be wrong, and for the same reason. In any way, to disagree with him, or any other of the saintly theologians of the Church, on an undefined matter of the Faith, is certainly not presumptuous."[125] If St. Thomas were alone in holding this doctrine, perhaps they would have a leg to stand on; but St. Thomas is in union with St. Cypri-

---

[120] Bro. Michael, letter of March 3, 1986.
[121] Dz. 388: Pope Innocent III.
[122] "Reply to Verbum," *Res Fidei,* February 1987, p.9.
[123] Bro. Michael, letter of March 3, 1986.
[124] *After the Boston Heresy Case,* Gary Potter, p.203.
[125] *Op. cit.*, p.106

an, St. Augustine, St. Ambrose, St. Prosper, St. John Chrysostom, St. Bede, St. Bernard, St. Albert the Great, St. Bonaventure, St. Robert Bellarmine, St. Alphonsus Liguori, Pope Innocent III, Pope Eugene IV, Pope Pius IX, Pope St. Pius X, Pope Benedict XV, *etc.*, with not a single one on the opposite side! Aren't the followers of Fr. Feeney ashamed to find themselves opposing so many holy Doctors and popes?

Secondly, they claim that this teaching is not infallible. Do they claim that one is free to reject that which has not been infallibly defined? That would be explicitly against an infallible decree of Vatican I:

> Moreover, by divine and Catholic faith everything ***must be believed*** that is contained in the written word of God or in tradition, and that is proposed by the Church as a divinely revealed object of belief either in a solemn decree ***or in her ordinary, universal magisterium*** (Dz. 1792).

This teaching being part of the *Ordinary and Universal Magisterium* of the Church, it is part of the deposit of Faith, which each Catholic ought to hold fast faithfully! One is NOT entitled to reject a unanimous teaching of the Magisterium under the mere pretext that it has not be defined; otherwise, you would reject the condemnation of contraception, the impossibility of ordination of women, *etc*. These are similar examples of unanimous teachings of the ordinary magisterium of the Church, yet undefined: these teachings are obligatory, not optional.

Thirdly, they bring long lists of quotes of popes, Fathers and Doctors on the necessity of belonging to the Catholic Church or on the necessity of the sacrament of baptism, ***pretending that these quotes reject baptism of blood and baptism of desire***. A typical example of this is *The Apostolic Digest*, by Michael Malone: under the title "Neither baptism of desire nor baptism of blood suffices for salvation," he does not dare to give a single quote of the many saints we have quoted, but he quotes other passages of the same saints and doctors AS IF these passages were against baptism of desire and baptism of blood. Upon reading this, one is appalled at the dishonesty of the man: if he were honestly interested in presenting the teaching of the saints on a subject, such as baptism of desire, he ought to put what they said about it! He ought not to let the reader erroneously think that these saints were against it, when he knows perfectly that these saints taught it explicitly! But by the very misleading title of his chapter, he changes the meaning of the quotes he aligns afterwards, *as if* they were opposed to baptism of blood and baptism of desire. Hence the following dilemma, put in an Open Letter to Brother Francis, on December 11, 1999 (no answer was ever received).

THE DILEMMA

In your December bulletin *Mancipia*, you pretend to refute Fr. Rulleau's excellent study on *Baptism of Desire: A Patristic Commentary*.[126] You have **no other defense** than to pretend there is a contradiction in St. Augustine, St. Ambrose, not to mention all the other Doctors of the Church[127] who all professed both the necessity of baptism and the existence of baptism of blood and baptism of desire. Now none of these Doctors saw a contradiction in their doctrine. Therefore you are faced with the dilemma:

Either there is objectively a contradiction, an incompatibility between the necessity of baptism as the Church holds it, and the doctrine on baptism of blood and baptism of desire. In this case all these Doctors were blind, incapable of seeing this contradiction, no matter how clever and how much praised by the Church they may be; all the theologians at least in the second millennium have been unanimously blind and also incapable of seeing that contradiction; only Fr. Feeney and his followers have been found more clever than all the Doctors and theologians and were the first to discover such contradiction.

Or there is no objective contradiction, the two teachings are compatible.

But you would object: "the Council of Trent's canons on baptism clearly contradict the Angelic Doctor." Here again you are faced with the same dilemma:

---

[126] Published by *Angelus Press*.
[127] They are many! Just for memory: St. Bernard, St. Bonaventure, St. Thomas Aquinas, St. Robert Bellarmine, St. Alphonsus Liguori, *etc.*, plus many Popes and Fathers of the Church, as early as St. Cyprian. One should add those who teach explicitly Baptism of Blood, though they were silent on Baptism of Desire: indeed from their own admission, Fr. Feeney's teaching on the necessity of the character of baptism is incompatible with the doctrine on baptism of blood, too.

Either there is an objective contradiction, incompatibility between the Canons of the Council of Trent as the Church understands them, and the doctrine of the Angelic Doctor on baptism of desire. In this case, it was seen by none of the Bishops members of the Council of Trent,[128] none of the most famous Saints who applied the Council of Trent such as St. Charles Borromeo and St. Robert Bellarmine, who both hold baptism of desire. The teaching of the holy Doctors posterior to the Council of Trent thought St. Thomas Aquinas's doctrine on baptism of desire so little in opposition with the Council of Trent that St. Alphonsus Liguori affirms that the doctrine on baptism of desire is *"de fide*–of Faith," *basing himself explicitly on the Council of Trent!* The Canon Law itself prepared by St. Pius X teaches that catechumens ought to be given ecclesiastical burial. Thus all of these saints, Doctors, holy popes were wrong, and at last came Fr. Feeney who was first to see.

Or there is no objective contradiction.

There is no way you can escape these dilemma: either all these Saints were right and you are wrong, or they were all wrong and you alone are right. I know a follower of Fr. Feeney who did not fear to write that they were all wrong. I hope you realize the enormity of such a claim, and correct yourself.

Not only given the respect due to the holy Fathers of the Church, holy Doctors and popes, but above all given the fact that the unanimous Tradition of the Church is the sure sign that a doctrine belongs to the deposit of Faith, every Catholic is bound in conscience–as soon as he knows that so many Fathers, Doctors, popes and saints have taught both–to hold that both the necessity of Baptism and the doctrine on Baptism of Blood and Baptism of Desire are not in contradiction, but rather are both necessary to understand properly the dogma "outside the Church there is no salvation."

---

[128] The Council Fathers at Trent had put St. Thomas Aquinas's *Summa Theologica* on the altar, together with the Holy Bible, to be their reference book for sound doctrine.

ANSWER TO ADDITIONAL OBJECTIONS OF FR. FEENEY

THE PRECISE ERROR OF FR. FEENEY

The error in Fr. Feeney's excessive reaction precisely lies in this, that, though he admitted that God could infuse sanctifying grace before baptism, yet he said: "God would not allow one to die in the state of grace, but not yet baptized." "Fr. (Feeney) taught that God would have seen to it that those few martyrs who were reported to have died without baptism would not have left this life without baptism."[129]

Such an affirmation makes liars of the very persons who reported the martyrdom of these martyrs! This is a gratuitous affirmation, in opposition to the first-hand knowledge and teaching of the Fathers, as seen above. Remember St. Cyprian went through three persecutions: he knew personally many martyrs and confessors; when he speaks of "catechumens apprehended before their baptism and slain for the name of Christ," he does not speak in the air. He knew some of them personally.

Fr. Feeney himself was aware of the novelty of this very opinion of his, thinking that on this point he was "improving *(sic)* upon the teaching of some of the Doctors."[130]

In the *Bread of Life,* p.137, Fr. Feeney wrote:

> Q. What are we to say to those who believe there are such souls [souls that die in the state of justification but have not received baptism of water]?
>
> A. We must say to them that they are making reason prevail over Faith, and the laws of probability over the Providence of God.

The answer should rather be: We must say that they make the teachings of the Fathers of the Church, of the Doctors of the

---

[129] Letter to Dr. Coomaraswamy, February 3, 1983.
[130] Bro. Michael, *ibid.*

Church, of the popes and saints prevail upon the "improvements" of Fr. Feeney!

Why not simply accept the teaching of St. Cyprian, St. Cyril of Jerusalem, St. Ambrose, St. Augustine, St. Fulgentius, St. Bernard, Pope Innocent III, St. Bonaventure, St. Thomas Aquinas, the Council of Trent, St. Robert Bellarmine, St. Catherine of Siena, St. Alphonsus, Pope Pius IX, Pope St. Pius X, Pope Benedict XV, *etc.*, that there are such souls in heaven?

Instead of presumptuously "improving upon the teaching of some Doctors" let us rather humbly "hold fast to the doctrine of the Fathers"![131]

Do Not Confuse Sanctifying Grace and Character

Let us first make some simple clarifications. The word grace is very widely used in the Holy Scripture and in the Church's teaching. In its wide meaning, it signifies any free gift of God, and more particularly, any free gift of God in the supernatural order. Thus we speak of the grace of faith, or of the grace of being born in a Catholic family, *etc.* The greatest of these supernatural gifts inherent to our soul is sanctifying grace ("the state of grace") which is a participation in the life of God: "He hath made us partakers of the divine nature" (II Pet. 1:4). It cannot be had without the virtues of faith, hope and charity. The just men in the Old Testament had this sanctifying grace, though they did not have the character of baptism.

According to St. Thomas Aquinas, sanctifying grace is the interior bond of the Church, because it is it that makes us united with Christ *in act* (*ST,* III, Q.8, A.3), as a living member of His Mystical Body. St. Thomas does not speak of the exterior bond, which is the direct consequence of this interior bond. Indeed, from this triple interior bond of faith, hope and charity flow the exterior bonds: interior faith leads to the profession of faith; hope leads to prayer, hence the union of worship which is principally found in the sacraments, the door of them being baptism and the summit being the Holy Sacrifice of the Mass; charity leads to obedience, hence the bond of ecclesiastical communion. Here we

---

[131] Dz. 388: Pope Innocent III speaking precisely about baptism of desire! See p.43.

meet the definition of the Church given by St. Robert Bellarmine, as we have seen above.

All the above study of the Fathers and Doctors manifests that the Church always held that the interior bond with the Catholic Church is absolutely necessary *in re* for salvation: the exterior bond with the Catholic Church is necessary *re aut voto–in fact or in desire* for salvation. But the exterior bond is necessary for the *complete* belonging to the Catholic Church on earth.

In sacramental theology, the expression *the grace of a sacrament* has a very special meaning: it signifies the ultimate effect of the sacrament in the soul, that is, the reception or the increase of sanctifying grace with a particular fruitfulness in the practice of the virtues related with that sacrament (such as fortitude for the sacrament of confirmation). Thus the Catechism teaches that a sacrament is an outward sign instituted by Christ to give grace.[132] They produce the grace that they signify. All the sacraments give grace, if received with the proper dispositions. Sanctifying grace being the life of the soul, five sacraments are called *sacraments of the living*, because they must be received already in the state of grace, which they increase; and two sacraments, *viz.*, baptism and penance, are called *sacraments of the dead*, because they are made to give or restore the state of grace to those who have it not, and thus were in the state of spiritual death.

The sacramental character is an entirely different reality. Only three sacraments imprint a character. It is imprinted in the soul, even if received with improper disposition. It remains in the soul even if one goes to hell. Thus the character is not a participation in the life of Christ, since the damned have no share in that life at all. What is it? St. Thomas explains to us that it is a certain "deputation to a spiritual service pertaining to the worship of God according to the rite of the Christian religion" (*ST,* III, Q.63, A.2). Thus its purpose and necessity is for the Church on earth, though it remains in the next life, in heaven for the glory of those who have worthily fulfilled this deputation, and in hell for the shame of those who have been unfaithful to it.

---

[132] *Baltimore Catechism,* Q.136.

Now a sacrament may belong to the Divine worship in three ways: first in regard to the thing done; secondly, in regard to the agent; thirdly, in regard to the recipient. In regard to the thing done, the Eucharist belongs to the Divine worship, for the Divine worship consists principally therein, so far as it is the sacrifice of the Church. And by this same sacrament a character is not imprinted on man; because it does not ordain man to any further sacramental action or benefit received, since rather is it "the end and consummation of all the sacraments," as Dionysius says (*Eccl. Hier.* iii). But it contains within itself Christ, in Whom there is not the character, but the very plenitude of the Priesthood.

But it is the sacrament of order that pertains to the sacramental agents: for it is by this sacrament that men are deputed to confer sacraments on others: while the sacrament of Baptism pertains to the recipients, since it confers on man the power to receive the other sacraments of the Church; whence it is called the "door of the sacraments." In a way Confirmation also is ordained for the same purpose, as we shall explain in its proper place. Consequently, these three sacraments imprint a character, namely, Baptism, Confirmation, and Order (*ST*, III, Q.63, A.6).

There is a spiritual danger in Fr. Feeney's over-insistence on the character of baptism. This character is indelible, we cannot make it grow. So this over-insistence can lead to spiritual apathy: well, I have my seal, I have fulfilled the requirements for salvation, I do not have to worry any more! On the contrary, the Church teaches that sanctifying grace can grow, and it can be lost, too: "Forgetting the things that are behind and stretching forth myself to those that are before, I press towards the mark, to the prize of the supernal vocation of God in Christ Jesus" (Phil. 3:13, 14). This is proper Catholic spirituality, not based on a false security of an indelible character, but on the dynamic of a participation of the divine life of Christ in us!

Desiring to insist on the necessity of the (exterior sign of the) sacrament of baptism, Fr. Feeney and his disciples have practically bestowed upon the character of baptism what the popes, Doctors, and all the Catholic theologians say of the grace of baptism (in the strict sense), which grace is received by those who have "baptism of desire." Thus Fr. Feeney or his followers were led to teach confusing things about the character of baptism.

1. "The character is itself a sanctifying grace"![133] The sacramental character is certainly a gift of God (grace, in its wide meaning), and it is useful for our sanctification (sanctifying), but the practice of the Church has been to reserve the combined appellation of sanctifying grace to a reality different from the character, and superior to it. To make a comparison, each divine Person is holy, and each one is a spirit, but the combined appellation "Holy Spirit–*Spiritus Sanctus*" has been reserved by the practice of Our Lord and of the Church to signify the Third Person, not without deep reasons. Let us follow and respect the practice of the Church and avoid confusion. Thus in the context of sacramental theology, the above affirmation of Fr. Feeney's followers is utmost confusion, in opposition to the common teaching of the Doctors of the Church!

Bro. Robert Mary[134] in his response to the first edition acknowledges the correctness of the above, but falls into further confusion: "The character is a grace called *gratia gratis data*, an abiding disposition, freely given, which assists a mature Catholic in his efforts to regain or increase in holiness." Now the term *gratia gratis data* means the charismata, such as the gift of prophecy or of miracles: the character is certainly not such! Indeed charismata are not given to each and every Christian, but only according to the choice of God to a few, mostly some chosen saints. The charismata are not made for the personal sanctification of the one who has it, but for the common edification of the Church. On the contrary, the character of baptism is intended for everyone (everyone ought to be baptized), and it is for his own personal sanctification. I have never seen any theologian confusing character and charisma!

2. The baptismal character is "the seal without which one is lacking the essential incarnational anointment marking him as heir of the heavenly kingdom."[135] This is new theology, and not in

---

[133] "Reply to Verbum," *Res Fidei*, February 1987, p.22.
[134] *Op. cit.*, pp.192-103.

conformity with past Catholic doctrine. The "essential" requirement to be "heir of the heavenly kingdom" is "sanctifying grace," which is a participation in the divine life of Christ, it is the living image of Christ in our soul ("incarnational anointment"):

> For the Spirit himself giveth testimony to our spirit, that we are the sons of God. And if sons, heirs also, heirs indeed of God, and joint heirs with Christ: yet so, if we suffer with him, that we may be also glorified with him (Rom. 8:16, 17).

The character remains even if one falls into mortal sin; how could such a one still be "heir of the heavenly kingdom"? By his sin, he has lost any title to heaven. No, it is not the character that makes *heir of God*, but rather sanctifying grace.

Conformity with Christ is required. St. Paul said: "For whom he foreknew, he also predestinated to be made conformable to the image of his Son" (Rom. 8:29). But this conformity with Christ is by *faith working through charity* (Gal. 5:6), according to the same St. Paul: "Be ye therefore imitators of God, as most dear children: and walk in love, as Christ also hath loved us and hath delivered himself for us, an oblation and a sacrifice to God for an odor of sweetness" (Eph. 5:1, 2).

3. "Let us suppose a man receives baptism sinfully...he is freed from original sin! Does he go into a state of justification? He does not!"[136] This also is new theology. Such a man certainly does not go into a state of justification, but he is not even freed from original sin, though he received the character of baptism. No sin, not even original sin, can be forgiven without the infusion of grace,[137] to which that man puts an obstacle by remaining attached to some grievous sin. The character of baptism is not incompatible with sin (it even exists in the damned in hell), it was thus received. But remission of original sin (or of any sin) cannot be done as long as there is an attachment to mortal sin: original sin would then be forgiven by a good confession, if that man makes one afterwards.

---

[135] "Reply to Verbum," *Res Fidei,* February 1987, p.19.
[136] *Bread of Life,* p.132.
[137] *ST,* I-II, Q.113, A.2.

Bro. Robert Mary[138] thinks he responds to the above by bringing a text of Innocent III, but that text only states that fear, like bad dispositions, does not make the sacrament of baptism invalid, hence the "character of Christianity" is imprinted. But he falsely concludes: "he receives the sacrament, with *all* of its effects." Not so. Bad dispositions are an obstacle to grace, and in an infallible canon, the Council of Trent declares:

> If anyone says that the sacraments of the New Law do not contain the grace that they signify, or that they do not confer that grace *upon those who do not place any obstacle in the way...* let him be anathema! (Session 6, Canon 6).

The Council does not speak here of *obstacles that invalidate the sacrament*, but obstacles to the production of grace. Hence the Church has always taught that the sacrament of baptism properly given outside the Church is valid, imprints a character, but does not confer grace. Bro. Robert Mary, by claiming against proper theology that "the grace is given to all who are validly baptized," is led to conclude: "the heretic receives the remission of all sin, original and actual sins committed prior to his Baptism." Now this is explicitly opposed to the dogma taught by Boniface VIII in *Unam Sanctam*: "Outside this Church there is no salvation and no remission of sins!"

The Church teaches that baptized heretics only receive grace and forgiveness of sins when, returning to the Catholic Church, they are absolved by the sacrament of penance from their sins. Do they have to confess original sin? No, since the matter of the sacrament of penance is the sins committed after baptism. What happens is this: through the confession of heresy and of the sacrilegious reception of baptism (and of the sins from then on), all sins from the time of baptism are forgiven in virtue of the absolution, and all sins prior to baptism (including original sin) are forgiven in virtue of the very sacrament of baptism which can *then* bring its fruits, since the "obstacle in the way" spoken of by Trent is now removed.

---

[138] The references in this passage are from *Can Only Baptized Roman Catholics Enter into Heaven*, pp.195, 198, 199.

4. Bro. Robert Mary accuses: "Fr. Laisney completely disregards the traditional teaching of the Church on the ***necessity of the baptismal seal*** impressed only by the sacrament."[139] I challenge him to show it! The Church in her documents is very careful to place the absolute necessity ***precisely not on the sacrament of faith, but on the faith of the sacrament*** as we have seen above (see Innocent III, p.43, and the Council of Trent in footnote 70). This is because that which is *absolutely* necessary is sanctifying grace (faith living through charity), and not the exterior sacrament. This one (and its character) is necessary *relatively* to this sanctifying grace and not by itself. Thus it is necessary *re aut voto*. Truly, the followers of Fr. Feeney say of the baptismal character that which the Church teaches of baptismal grace, *i.e.*, sanctifying grace.

5. "The 'desire for baptism,' if properly made, may put a person in the state of sanctifying grace. If the person perseveres in and dies in that state, he still cannot enter the kingdom of God. He lacks the one thing that only the sacrament can provide–the indelible mark or spiritual character imprinted on his soul."[140] That goes explicitly against the Council of Trent saying that "the justified have everything necessary for them," as we shall see now.

JUSTIFICATION AND SALVATION

Since the Council of Trent teaches that baptism was "necessary for justification...*re aut voto*–in fact or in desire," it is clear that the character of baptism is not absolutely necessary for justification. Thus Fr. Feeney taught that the character of baptism was absolutely necessary, not for justification, but for salvation.

The distinction between justification and salvation is classic in the Church's teaching: Justification is the passage from the state of sin to the state of grace; salvation is the passage from the state of grace in this world to the state of glory in heaven (either directly or through purgatory). Thus justification is the beginning of the spiritual life, salvation is its end.

---

[139] *Op. cit.*, p.202.
[140] Bro. Robert Mary, *op. cit.*, pp.116, 117.

Baptism is the sacrament of the beginning of spiritual life[141]: it is a birth. If that life is later lost by mortal sin, it can be recovered by the sacrament of penance, which is thus like a spiritual resurrection: it was indeed instituted by Our Lord Jesus Christ on the day of His Resurrection.

Bro. Robert Mary erroneously writes: "All sacraments justify."[142] No, only baptism and penance.[143] The others must be received in the state of grace: they increase that grace, but do not give it. If one receives them without the state of grace, far from being justified, he adds a sin of sacrilege to his previous ones.

It follows clearly that baptism is the sacrament of justification. To claim the sacrament of baptism necessary "for salvation, not for justification" is to misplace it at the end rather than at the beginning of the spiritual life. No, we should rather hold with the Council of Trent that the sacrament of baptism (of water) is necessary for justification, *re aut voto*–in fact or in desire. Baptism is necessary for salvation because and only because it is necessary for justification. Thus it is necessary for salvation in the same way as it is necessary for justification, *re aut voto*–in fact or in desire.[144]

What then is needed for salvation? Perseverance in the state of grace: "He that shall persevere to the end, he shall be saved" (Mt. 24:13). In one word, to die in the state of grace is necessary and

---

[141] St. Thomas wrote: "Baptism is the beginning of the spiritual life, and the door of the sacraments, whereas the Eucharist is, as it were, the consummation of the spiritual life." See p.38.

[142] *Op. cit.*, p.202.

[143] Exceptionally, Extreme Unction for someone contrite for his sins but too sick to be able to confess them could also restore sanctifying grace.

[144] Bro. Robert Mary pretends that here we "circumvent" Canon 5 of the Council of Trent, which says: "If anyone says that Baptism is optional, that is, not necessary unto salvation, let him be anathema." But, as the honest reader can see, we do not say that it is not necessary; we say **with the Council of Trent** that it is ***necessary re aut voto***! Bro. Robert Mary's criticism on this chapter is of the same kind: it falls off the mark, it is not to the point. And his last one turns against him: indeed, he who "constructs premises from which it follows that dogmas are historically false or dubious" (decree *Lamentabili*) is not me, but rather Fr. Feeney, from whose faulty exegesis and construed premises on the baptismal character it follows that the Church erred in teaching baptism of blood and desire, and had a false understanding of the dogma *extra Ecclesiam nulla salus*.

sufficient to be saved. Now, perseverance includes the fulfillment of one's duties. Thus if one neglects to receive the sacrament of baptism (or of confession), he loses the grace he may have received through baptism of desire (or perfect contrition), as the Fathers and Doctors have so well said above.

This is exactly what the Council of Trent teaches:

> It is necessary to believe that *the justified have everything necessary for them* to be regarded as having completely satisfied the divine law for this life by their works, at least those which they have performed in God. And they may be regarded as having likewise truly merited *the eternal life they will certainly attain in due time, if they but die in the state of grace...*[145]

The distinction between justification and salvation is easily understood with the Old Testament: the Hebrews were slaves in Egypt, image of the kingdom of Satan, of the state of sin. They were delivered from it by the crossing of the Red Sea. But they were not yet in the promised land: they had to walk forty years, following Moses, and still had to cross the Jordan, and only then entered into the promised land. The crossing of the Red Sea is the image of baptism;[146] the crossing of the Jordan is the image of the death of the just. In between you have the whole Christian life, of fidelity to Christ and walking in the path of the commandments of God.

In the *Bread of Life*, Fr. Feeney teaches that salvation requires more than perseverance in the state of grace, that it requires something of "flesh and blood," and he concludes that this thing of "flesh and blood" required for salvation is the water of baptism: "Justification is now being turned into salvation with the aid of water" (p.118). He concludes (p.25): "It is now: baptism of water, or damnation! If you do not desire that water, you cannot be justified. And if you do not get it, you cannot be saved."

Not only is it false to say, "justification is now being turned into salvation with the aid of water," but it is also very dangerous for the spiritual life and leads to Protestantism! Indeed, as seen

---

[145] Sess. 6, Chap. 16, Dz. 809, TCT 573.
[146] According to St. Paul: "All our Fathers were baptized in the cloud and in the sea" (I Cor. 10:2).

above, salvation is at the end of spiritual life; now the reception of the water of baptism is certainly not the end of the spiritual life! Does not the priest say to the newly baptized at the end of the ceremony of baptism: "Keep your baptism above reproach. Keep the commandments of God, so that when the Lord comes to His marriage feast, you may meet him in the halls of heaven with all His saints." In other words, you are not yet arrived, you still have to walk on the path of the commandments of God. To let the people think that, with the water, their "justification has been turned into salvation" leads them to think that they have reached the end, they have nothing else to do: once saved, always saved. This is true of the entry into heaven— once there, always there— but it is not true of the grace of baptism: it can be lost.

The Council of Trent affirms that these *incarnational requirements* are given to the soul *in justification*:

> For, although no one can be just, but he to whom the merits of the passion of our Lord Jesus Christ are communicated, yet *is this done in the said justification* of the impious when by the merit of the same holy passion, the charity of God is poured forth, by the Holy Spirit, in the hearts (Rom. 5:5) of those that are justified, and is inherent therein: whence, man, through Jesus Christ *in whom he is ingrafted*, receives, *in the said justification*, together with the remission of sins, all these (gifts) infused at once, faith, hope, charity.[147]

For these "Incarnational requirements" for justification itself, one needs the waters of baptism, *re aut voto*–in fact or at least in desire, as Trent teaches.

Fr. Feeney wrote: "…the sinners, just and unjust,…"[148] There is no such thing as a just sinner! Such a statement manifests an erroneous understanding of justification!

Unfulfilled and fulfilled Justice

Fr. Feeney says: "Unfulfilled justice is the state of justification.[149] Fulfilled justice is the state of salvation."[150] That "unful-

---

[147] Sess. 6, Chap. 7, Dz. 800, TCT 564.
[148] *Bread of Life*, p.16.
[149] There is no such thing as a "state of justification." Justification is defined by Trent as a *passage*, not a state!
[150] *Bread of Life*, p.118.

filled justice" by sanctifying grace, would be "fulfilled" by the "sacrament of water."[151]

It is true that after justification, there remain here below the wounds of original sin and of our own personal sins: due to these wounds, one can say that the state of grace is unfulfilled justice; these wounds are healed by the practice of the Christian duties (prayer, reception of penance and Holy Eucharist, good works and mortification); if they are not completely healed here below, one must pass through purgatory to obtain this "fulfilled justice." But there is no state of salvation here below! The Church explicitly taught that these wounds are not completely healed by the water of baptism themselves.[152] Thus one does not enter a state of fulfilled justice by the waters of baptism! If one with baptism of desire is prevented without fault on his part from receiving the sacrament of baptism, he did not fail to fulfill his duties, and thus can be saved, though most probably through purgatory.

They base this distinction between unfulfilled and fulfilled justice on Mt. 3:15 where our Lord asks to be baptized by St. John the Baptist, and says: "Suffer it to be so now. For so it becometh us to fulfill all justice." But this is a new interpretation of these words; the Fathers interpreted them as an act of perfect humility of Our Lord, model of humility for all; St. Augustine says that Our Lord here gave an example of humility to the great of this world, that they do not disdain to receive His baptism, since He Himself did not disdain John's baptism.

Moreover, fulfillment comes from what is more perfect: what is more perfect fulfils what is less perfect. Now it has been the constant teaching of the Church that sanctifying grace, by which a soul is pleasing to God, is more perfect than the character of the sacraments, which can and does remain in the sinner. The Church teaches that some spiritual gifts of God can remain in the soul, even after one has lost sanctifying grace by mortal sin: thus one can retain the virtue of faith, even of hope, after having lost charity. One retains the characters even in hell. But none of these spiritual gifts is sufficient to open heaven for us without sanctifying grace and charity! Thus the character without grace is not suf-

---

[151] Bro. Michael, March 3, 1986.
[152] Council of Trent, in an *ex cathedra* Canon, Dz. 792.

ficient; it is sanctifying grace that brings to perfection the soul sealed with the character, not the contrary.

Moreover, it is also the constant teaching that Christian perfection consists in the perfection of charity,[153] *i.e.,* in a perfect love of God and of our neighbor. St. Paul says that charity is the "bond of perfection" (Col. 3:14). The Church teaches that baptism of blood is more perfect than baptism of water precisely because it includes a perfect act of charity: "Greater love than this no man hath, that a man lay down his life for his friends" (Jn. 15:13).

WERE SOME MIRACLES PERFORMED TO PROVE THE NECESSITY OF BAPTISM OF WATER?

God did indeed perform some miracles, right from the beginning of the Church, to manifest the necessity of the grace of baptism: in the Acts of the Apostles (8:26-40) the Deacon Philip is miraculously warned to go and evangelize the eunuch of the Queen of Ethiopia, whom he baptized, and then was "rapt" by the Spirit back into his place. The lives of the saints have similar and even more spectacular examples.

But a miracle is not opposed to another miracle! It is not because God performed one kind of miracle that He does not perform other kinds of miracles. Let us consider a similar case: it belongs to the natural law that one must eat to sustain his own life. God performed a miracle sending the prophet Habacuc to Daniel in the lions' den in order to bring him some food (Dan. 14:32-38). Similarly, God sent ravens to bring Elias some bread and meat in the desert (III Kg. 17:6.); yet the fact that God miraculously brought the natural food to His prophets does not mean that God did not also miraculously sustain the life of some saints without food (*e.g.,* St. Nicolas de Flüe, Theresa Newmann...).

All these miracles perfectly fit the divine power and goodness: it perfectly fits that Christ supports the predication of his missionaries and His law of baptism by performing miracles to provide the exterior sacrament of baptism to some souls (see Acts 8:26-40). It also perfectly fits that Christ supports the truth of His own words: "Ask and ye shall receive..." (Mt. 7:7), and of the beautiful prayer "Never was it known that any one who fled to thy

---

[153] *ST,* II-II, Q.184, A.1.

protection, implored thy help or sought thy intercession was left unaided!" by granting the prayer of His Mother at the request of Fr. Augustine Marie of the Blessed Sacrament[154] for the conversion and salvation of his mother by baptism of desire.

Therefore do not argue one miracle of God against another!

NECESSITY OF THE MAGISTERIUM OF THE CHURCH

The argument goes thus: a fallible magisterium is not capable of proposing the truths of Faith in such a way that we adhere to them absolutely as we ought to adhere to the truth revealed by God. Only an infallible magisterium can do so. Now such a magisterium is found only in the Catholic Church. Therefore, outside the Catholic Church there is no supernatural virtue of Faith possible.

The first answer is to note that this does not apply to catechumens, since they received the teaching of the Faith from the Catholic Church! So this is not an objection against baptism of blood and baptism of desire for explicit catechumens.

We concede that any other "churches," including the Orthodox churches, not having such an infallible magisterium, are not adequate channels of Divine Revelation, so as to assure the *motive* of Faith, which is on the authority of God, which is not found in these churches. They present the *object* of Faith, but not with the *authority* required for an assent of Faith. How could one know that the Scriptures come from God, if it is not presented by a Church speaking in the name of God, with a special mission to teach? Our Lord gave this mission to His living apostles: "Go, teach all nations..." This mission is continued from century to century in that Church which has been founded by Christ, not among those who separated themselves from it. Thus any church that cannot show her historical link with Christ–her *apostolicity*– cannot speak with the authority of Christ.

The conclusion from the above is that no other church can be a *means of salvation*, contrary to what the innovators of Vatican II say.

However, that does not prevent God from giving special interior lights that give together both the knowledge of the object to

---

[154] See first example, p.84.

be believed, and the absolute certitude of its divine source. St. Thomas Aquinas teaches this explicitly, and his teaching has been followed on this point by the Church:

> We must hold very certainly that God would reveal to him *either through an internal inspiration* those truths that ought to be believed, or would send him a preacher of the Faith, as He sent Peter to Cornelius.[155]

Someone knowing the *object* of Faith through a false religion could receive such light. But then this light, when faithfully received, casts away the darkness of the errors of that false religion, and such a person is no longer *formally* of that false religion, but rather like a catechumen of the Catholic Church. But do not misunderstand me: Protestants claim that each one has such lights; however, Our Lord has told us: "by their fruits you shall know them." We recognize that such *an internal inspiration* comes from the Holy Ghost when its object is the Catholic Faith, and we recognize that it does *not* come from the Holy Ghost when its object is not in conformity with the Catholic Faith. Hence Protestants are wrong to claim such lights against the true Faith. But that does not exclude that God does give such lights to whom He wills.

WHAT IS THE NECESSITY OF THE EXTERIOR BELONGING TO THE CHURCH?

Given the nature of man, body and soul, and above all given the very mystery of the Incarnation, the exterior belonging to the Church naturally accompanies its interior belonging. To deny the importance of the exterior belonging to the Mystical Body of Christ, is akin to the denial of the visibility of the Church, and akin to the denial of the Incarnation.

A man can live without a foot, yet his body is not complete without it. A saint can be in heaven without his body, yet his beatitude is not complete without the resurrection of the body; his beatitude is perfect, though not complete: it is perfect because the glorification of his body is not going to give him a more excellent bliss, but it is not complete because his body is an integral part of himself.

---

[155] *De Veritate*, Q.14, A.11, ad 1.

In a similar way, men with baptism of desire have the life of Christ in them (by grace), which is the most important thing, the essential requirement for going to heaven; they are joined with Christ according to St. Paul: "Whosoever are led by the Spirit of God, they are the sons of God. And if sons, heirs also; heirs indeed of God, and joint heirs with Christ" (Rom. 8:14,17). Their union with God is perfect, yet it is not complete: the exterior union would not bring them something more important or more perfect than the interior union with Christ, but it brings an integral part of the life with Christ. Hence in the long list of testimonies from Fathers, Doctors or theologians in this book, it is clear that they consider that those with baptism of desire are members of the Mystical Body of Christ, being bound with Christ by sanctifying grace, though their bond is not complete.

It belongs to the very nature of charity to love not only Christ the Head of His Body, but also all the members of Christ. Would a fiancé say to his fiancée, "I love your head but not your body?" (Hence, those who do not love and honor the saints, do not have charity; it is a very simple test, just ask some Protestant: "Do you love the saints?") Therefore, anyone who, by the grace of the Holy Ghost, is given the virtues of faith, hope and charity, must desire and do all in his power to be in perfect and complete union with all the members of Christ, *i.e.,* with His Church.

If he does not love the unity of the Church, he does not love Christ, who gave this unity to His Church.

Note that this love of the unity of the Church can be found in "good men expelled from the Christian Congregation by the turbulent seditions of carnal men...*Hos coronat in occulto Pater, in occulto videns*—The Father, who sees in secret, crowns these men in secret. This kind of man seems quite rare, though examples are not lacking; they are even more numerous than one could think."[156]

It is important to point out that it is not sufficient to say, "without the Church, no salvation," we must say with all the Tradition of the Church, "outside the Church, no salvation." One cannot say that one could be saved by the Church, though outside the Church. To be saved, it is not only necessary to receive grace from Christ, we must be in Christ by charity: "He that abideth in charity, abideth in God, and God in him" (I Jn. 4:16). Charity is received by baptism of desire. Now to be in Christ necessarily means to be in His Mystical Body, the Church, which is the Catholic Church. One must never forget that the actual graces of God given before the conversion precisely lead towards Jesus Christ and His Church; if one follows these actual graces with docility, he will succeed in finding Jesus Christ and His Church.

Thus we must conclude that the interior union with Christ and His Church by faith, hope and charity is absolutely necessary *in re*–in fact. But *the exterior union with the Church is necessary at least* **in voto**–*in desire*, when one does everything he can to have the exterior union with the Church, and when this exterior union is prevented by an obstacle uncontrollable and irremovable by his will. If that obstacle was not irremovable, and if he would neglect to remove it, then he would be guilty of this, and thus lose the grace of his baptism of desire.

Hence it is absolutely false to say: "Both Archbishop Lefebvre and Fr. Laisney think of the Church in the spiritual, invisible sense, to the exclusion of the visible sense, whenever her necessity for salvation is considered."[157]

But the reason for Bro. Robert Mary's error is that for him, "it is the sacramental character *alone* that incorporates one into the Roman Catholic Church."[158] No, not alone! It is only one of the bonds of the Church, and not the most important, since it can be had even outside the Church, even in hell! As a matter of fact, of the six bonds of the Church, it is the only one that remains in hell: indeed, no supernatural virtue remains there, nor the profession of the Catholic Faith, nor the submission to the Roman Pontiff; only the sacramental character! To pretend that "it is the sacramental character *alone* that incorporates one into the Roman

---

[156] St. Augustine, *De Vera Religione,* 11. In this passage, St. Augustine insists on the devotion of these good men "to keep and defend the Catholic Faith," and on the example of "their affection and sincere charity." Knowing how much St. Augustine stresses the importance of belonging to the unity of the Church, against the schism of Donatus, this passage reinforces the primacy of the interior union, sufficient to be "crowned by the Father" when exceptional circumstances prevent the exterior union. The application to the modern crisis of the Church and to the situation of Archbishop Lefebvre is left to the reader!
[157] Bro. Robert Mary, *op. cit.* p.217.
[158] Bro. Robert Mary, *op. cit.* p.204.

Catholic Church," manifests a very *mechanical* understanding of salvation. The Church's teaching is that it is essentially sanctifying grace, received normally in baptism of water, exceptionally in baptism of blood or desire, that incorporates one into the Roman Catholic Church. The sacrament of baptism received in the Church performs the complete incorporation into the Mystical Body of Christ, the Roman Catholic Church, because it includes all the six bonds of the Church: the profession of Faith (the rite itself is the first act of Catholic worship); the submission to this rite includes submission to the hierarchy; and above all because it gives sanctifying grace with the virtues of faith, hope and charity. We find here the definition of St. Robert Bellarmine: "the congregation of men bound together by the profession of the same Christian faith, and in the communion of the same sacraments, under the government of the legitimate shepherds, and chiefly of the one vicar of Christ on earth, the Roman Pontiff."[159] Note that St. Robert does not say a word on the sacramental character in this definition!

If the baptismal character were the *formal constitutive*[160] of the belonging to the Church, how could this character be found outside the Church, and even in hell? If it is not the *formal constitutive* of the belonging to the Church, then Fr. Feeney's whole position collapses. In fact, the baptismal character is a *sign of* the belonging to the Church, it is not *the belonging itself.*[161]

Is There a Loophole?

Fr. Feeney wanted to close all the loopholes which the Liberals were using to deny the dogma "outside the Church there is no

---

[159] See p.76.
[160] That is, *that which makes one a member* of the Church. Often Bro. Robert Mary attributes the incorporation into the Church to the baptismal character: "The Sacrament of Baptism is necessary for salvation primarily because of the baptismal character it impresses on the soul, by which a man is incorporated into Christ's Church" (*op. cit.* p.225). This is, as we said, to bestow upon the character that which the Church teaches of sanctifying grace. The truth is: the Sacrament of Baptism is necessary for salvation primarily because of *sanctifying grace* by which sins are forgiven, man becomes an adoptive child of God, a temple of the Holy Ghost, a living member of Christ and of His Church.

salvation." He thought baptism of desire to be such a loophole,[162] and this is why he rejected it. But it is not so! The objection presents baptism of desire as if it were an alternative for baptism of water, so that one would be allowed to choose between one or the other. But it is not so: baptism of desire can only be had by those who have chosen and desire with all their heart to receive baptism of water! Baptism of desire is not an option we can choose. Baptism of water is the only means that God has put in our power to receive justification. It is only in the power of God to give justification to some who have not yet received baptism of water.

Another way for the objection to present itself: the Church teaches that baptism of water is of necessity of means to be saved. Therefore one cannot be saved without it. The answer is simple: Baptism of water is of necessity of means to receive justification; therefore someone who has not yet received the grace of justification absolutely needs baptism of water. If God, who is not limited in His means, has already given this grace to someone before the reception of water, then baptism of water is no longer of necessity of means for that person (he has already received the ultimate fruit of baptism, which is the grace of a new spiritual birth), yet it is of necessity of precept. So either one absolutely needs or one is grievously bound to receive baptism of water: there is no loophole for man! If there is a loophole, it is for God, not for man!

---

[161] St. Augustine boldly says: Outside the Church, man can have the sacraments, but not salvation: "A man cannot have salvation, except in the Catholic Church. Outside the Catholic Church he can have everything except salvation. He can have honor, he can have sacraments, he can sing alleluia, he can answer amen, he can possess the gospel, he can have and preach faith in the name of the Father and of the Son and of the Holy Ghost; but never except in the Catholic Church will he be able to find salvation... He can even shed his blood [outside the Church], but not have the crown!" (Sermon to the people of the Church at Caesarea in Mauretania, No.6, R.J.,1858, BAC, 507, p.595).

[162] Bro. Robert Mary, *op. cit.* p.224: "If desire for Baptism is accepted as a substitute for the sacrament, the floodgates are opened, and the Dogma of Faith is completely washed away. The institution of the Church becomes meaningless!" One wonders, if this were true, how has it been possible that the Church has held baptism of desire for so many centuries, without having become meaningless!

At the root of this fear of a loophole, there is an inability to grasp the distinctions taught by the Church. The Doctors explained that there are several kinds of necessity: *1)* Metaphysical necessity, *i.e.*, necessity of nature, which God Himself cannot bypass, since it would imply contradiction. For instance, Christ cannot have a human nature without a human will. That is not a limitation on God, on the contrary, God is too intelligent to contradict Himself. *2)* Necessity of means: thus we have no other means to get sanctifying grace than baptism of water; yet God is not limited by the means He has established, and He can pour His grace without the water. Such bypassing of the laws He has established in the natural order is a miracle in nature; similarly baptism of desire is like a miracle in the supernatural order, possible but not common. *3)* Necessity of precept, which always requires the interior submission of the will, and the exterior fulfillment as much as one can. Not receiving with humble submission of the intellect these distinctions taught by the Church, they think that if one admits one exception to the baptism of water, then one makes it optional. For them either baptism of water is absolutely necessary or not necessary; if they hear of any exception, they feel the necessity of baptism is completely ruined and the dogma that outside the Church there is no salvation is ruined also. This is simply not true.

THE FUNDAMENTAL ERROR OF FR. FEENEY

We can see here that the fundamental error of Fr. Feeney is to follow his own interpretation of the dogma, and to re-interpret the Scriptures and the documents of the popes according to his own views. In one word, it is to put his views before the Church's teaching.

As fully documented in the section on the teaching of the Church, and as explained above, the proper understanding of the dogma of the Church *Extra Ecclesiam nulla salus* is that, in order to go to heaven, one must be united with the Roman Catholic Church *re aut voto*: the interior bond with the Church, which consists in sanctifying grace with Catholic faith, hope and charity, is absolutely necessary; the exterior bond with the Church, which consists in the profession of the Faith, the communion of worship and first of all the reception of the sacrament of baptism, and the hierarchical communion, is necessary *re aut voto*. As we have seen, the Fathers and Doctors never considered those baptized with their blood as being simply outside the Church, nor those "fervent catechumens" who were prevented by death: they belong to the Church, though their exterior bond is still incomplete. Hence, *the doctrine of baptism of blood and baptism of desire belongs to the proper understanding of the dogma.* To reject it is to reject the proper understanding of the dogma. It goes against Vatican I, which orders us: "Of the sacred dogmas, that sense must be faithfully upheld, which holy Mother Church has once declared; and one may never depart from this sense on the specious ground of a more profound understanding" (Dz. 1800). Isn't it precisely what Fr. Feeney did, pretending "to improve upon the Fathers"?

This attachment to one's own interpretation can lead some followers of Fr. Feeney to so stress the exterior belonging to the Church that they lose from sight the primacy of the interior union with Christ, attributing to the exterior sacrament what the Church says of the interior grace of the sacrament which, in exceptional cases, can be had without the exterior sacrament, though not without the desire of this external sacrament. As a consequence, they arrive at positions contradictory to the very definitions which they pretend to defend. An example: Fr. Wathen, after having given the passage of the Council of Trent on justification (which, as the Council says, can be had by baptism of desire), concludes:

> This disposition of soul and others equivalent to it...do bring justification. But, since such an act and disposition do not make one a member of the Church, they do not suffice for the reward of Heaven.[163]

Now, to pretend that one can be justified without being a member of the Church goes against Boniface VIII, who said that *outside the Church there is no remission of sins!* The truth is that we ought to consider that baptism of desire builds a first bond with Christ and His Church, an interior but real bond, which still must be completed by the exterior reception of the sacrament. However, thanks to that first bond with the Church, were such a

---

[163] *Who Shall Ascend*, p.109.

man to die before he could fulfill his will to be baptized, he could be saved.

St. Thomas, relying on St. Augustine, precisely refers to the primacy of the interior union with Christ in his article on the necessity of baptism, *Summa Theologica*, III, Q.68, A.2:

> *Sed contra:* St. Augustine wrote (*super* Levit. Q.84) that "the invisible sanctification has been given and has benefited to some without the visible sacraments; on the contrary the visible sanctification, consisting in the visible sacrament, can exist but not benefit without the invisible sanctification."[164]

Union with God is beautifully described by St. John: "God is charity: and he that abideth in charity, abideth in God, and God in him" (I Jn. 4:16). "Love therefore is the fulfilling of the law" (Rom. 13:10).

CAN FR. FEENEY AND HIS FOLLOWERS BE CALLED "HERETICS"?

The decree of excommunication of Fr. Feeney, approved and confirmed by Pope Pius XII on February 12, 1953, does not mention the charge of heretic, but rather that of a "grievous disobedience to the Authority of the Church." One cannot condemn them more than the Church did, so one should not say that they are formal "heretics."

However if, after one has explained to them properly the Catholic doctrine on baptism of desire (not the liberal doctrine), they publicly, stubbornly, "pertinaciously" refuse to correct themselves and "to hold fast to the doctrine of the Fathers" (Pope Innocent III), I cannot see how they could be excused of a grievous sin of temerity against the Faith, together with a sin of pride! Thus they could be denied Holy Communion.

WHAT ABOUT THE LETTER OF THE HOLY OFFICE TO CARDINAL CUSHING (JULY 27, 1949)?

The followers of Fr. Feeney make some controversy around this letter, due to the fact that it has been abusively interpreted by some as an opening for "salvation outside the Church." For in-

---

[164] Also, *ST*, III, Q.68, A.2, ad 1, see p.73.

stance, the headlines for the *Worcester Telegram*, a widely read Massachusetts newspaper, declared on September 2, 1949, "Vatican Rules Against Hub Dissidents: Holds No Salvation Outside Church Doctrine to Be False."[165]

However, instead of refusing to sign this letter, it seems to me that one should have rather shown how abusive such an interpretation is.

Indeed, the letter states unambiguously the necessity of "a supernatural faith" with "perfect charity."[166] In the light of this last paragraph, it becomes clear that "invincible ignorance" does not mean ignorance of all the truths of Faith, but rather of some particular ones such as the truth about baptism. If one does not take a passage of that letter out of its context (as the Liberals do), but rather reads it as a whole, especially in light of the last paragraph and of the whole previous pronouncements of the popes, Doctors and Fathers, it teaches pure Catholic doctrine!

In a similar way, if a Catholic author has an ambiguous statement, he should be interpreted in light of the whole of Catholic doctrine. For instance, Fr. Feeney "objected to that in the Baltimore Catechism which he foresaw as dangerous to the Faith,"[167] where the Catechism says:

> Q.632. Where will persons go who–such as infants–have not committed actual sin and who, through no fault of theirs, die without baptism?

This applies to all those who have never had the use of their reason, *i.e.,* infants and insane persons from birth. This does not apply to those who have had the use of their reason; indeed, St. Thomas teaches:

> When man begins to have the use of reason, he is not entirely excused from the guilt of venial or mortal sin. Now the first thing that occurs to a man to think about then, is to deliberate about himself. And if he then direct himself to the due end, he will, by means of grace, receive the remission of original sin: whereas if he does not then direct himself to the due end, as far

---

[165] Letter to the Holy Office, June 28, 1985.
[166] *The Church Teaches*, (Rockford, IL: TAN Books and Publishers, 1973) No.280.
[167] "Reply to Verbum," *Res Fidei,* February 1987, p.25.

as he is capable of discretion at that particular age, he will sin mortally, through not doing that which is in his power to do.[168]

The place where the unbaptized infants and insane go, is none other than the Limbo of the Infants; the expression "similar to" of the catechism is unfortunate, but certainly does not deserve the qualification of "dangerous to the Faith"!

Here it seems quite opportune to deplore that some good Catholic authors have some unfortunate expressions. When these expressions are taken in the context of their whole teaching, they can be understood in a good sense, thus the author should not be condemned, but his wording is sometime inappropriate.

For example: "Can a Protestant be saved? Yes, a Protestant can be saved if..."[169] Then the whole clause practically means: "if he has only the name of Protestant, though, through the grace of God, he has the reality of a Catholic!" The same content of doctrine should rather be expressed: "Can a Protestant be saved? No, a real Protestant cannot be saved. However it may happen that one has only the name of Protestant, but the reality of a Catholic through the grace of God." Indeed, Our Lord Jesus Christ said to the Pharisees: "Search the Scriptures, for you think in them to have life everlasting; and the same are they that give testimony of me!" (Jn. 5:39). As the Old Testament gives testimony to Jesus Christ, so the New Testament gives testimony to the Catholic Church, Mystical Body of Christ! Therefore, we can say in a similar way to Protestants: "Search the Scriptures, for you think in them to have life everlasting; and the same are they that give testimony of the Catholic Church, Mystical Body of Christ!" Now if a Protestant believes all of what the Holy Scriptures objectively say, not picking and choosing according to his private interpretation, then he believes the Catholic doctrine, and will be led, again by the grace of God, to the Catholic Church; and if he dies already putting in practice this doctrine, though before completely finding the Church, he may still be saved (this could happen for instance for a soul evangelized in a Communist country by a Protestant, with no opportunity to find the Catholic Church).

---

[168] *ST,* I-II, Q.89, A.6.
[169] Fathers Rumble and Carty, *Radio Replies,* (Rockford, IL: TAN Books and Publishers) Vol.1, Ch.9, No.539.

Another example: "Among Protestants, schismatics and pagans, there are souls which are really on the road to eternal life."[170] This whole booklet is quite good, but this sentence is not properly worded: the rest of the pamphlet manifests that the author means that some people *living among* Protestants, schismatics and pagans, yet, by the grace of God, *not adhering to* their Protestantism, schisms and paganism, but rather to those truths which God revealed to them, are on the road to heaven. The whole pamphlet makes it clear that the author does not mean that some real Protestants, real schismatics or real pagans are on the road to heaven!

Chronologically, it seems that Fr. Feeney suffered unjust persecution from liberal members of the US hierarchy in the post-World War II period because of his good stand for the dogma that outside the Catholic Church, there is no salvation. The letter of the Holy Office is dated 1949. It seems that it is only after having been unjustly persecuted, that he thought he should "improve upon the teaching of some of the Doctors." *The Bread of Life* in which he presents this new doctrine is dated 1952. Far from strengthening his position, this deviation from the teaching of the Doctors gave real motives to his opponents. Error is not a good weapon against error.

Conclusion

Our conclusion will be very simple. We have already repeated it many times in this section, because it is the heart of the question: Let us not pretend "to improve upon the teaching of some of the Doctors," but rather humbly "hold fast to the doctrine of the Fathers," of the popes, of the Doctors and of the saints, in all domains–in their interpretation of Holy Scripture, in their full adhesion to the dogma, Outside the Catholic Church there is no salvation, and to their doctrine on baptism of blood and of desire.

May the Blessed Virgin Mary help us to remain always faithful to the doctrine of the Church, and fervent to share it with many others, so that, by putting it in practice, we may be saved.

---

[170] Fr. J. Bainvel, S. J. *Is There Salvation Outside of the Catholic Church?* (Rockford, IL: TAN Books and Publishers) p.19.

APPENDIX I

Theologians

Billuart, O.P., *Summa Sancti Thomae*, tract. de Bapt., Ch.1, A.6, T.6 (Atrebati, 1968), pp.286-394.

The Catholic Encyclopedia, 1907, "Baptism," pp.265, 266 ; T.3, "Catechumen," p.431.

Catholic Dictionary, 1929, p.93.

Ferdinand Cavallera, *Thesaurus Doctrinae Catholicae*, No.266, 267, 1059 (Paris, 1936), pp.152, 153, 574.

Jules Corbet, *Histoire du Sacrement du Baptême* (Paris: Palmé, 1881), pp.148-156.

Dublanchy, *De Axiomate Extra Ecclesiam nulla salus* (Bar le Duc, 1895).

Fr. Joseph C. Fenton, "The Theological Proof for the Necessity of the Catholic Church" in the May 1948 issue of the *American Ecclesiastical Review*.

Card. Gaspari, *The Catholic Catechism*, p.194 (Latin edition).

J. P. Gury, S.J., *Compendium Theologiae Moralis*, T.2, No.234 (Rome, 1884), p.153.

Alexander of Hales, Part IV, Q. 8, M.9, A.4 (quoted by Franzelin).

Hervé, *Manuale Theologiae dogmatice*, T.1, No.342, 343, No.440 (Paris, 1935), pp.342-346, 446.

Père Edouard Hugon, O.P., *Hors de l'Eglise point de salut*, reprinted Fideliter (1995), pp.171, 190.

Hurter, *Compendium Theologicus*, (Innsbruck, 1891), T.3, p.276.

Fr. John Laux, *Mass and the Sacraments, A Course in Religion*, Book II (T.A.N., 1990), p.18.

Lehmkuhl, S.J., *Theologia Moralis*, T.2, No.55,56 (Herder, 1893), pp.43, 44.

H. Lennerz, S.J., *De Sacramento Baptismi* (1948), pp.91-125. He quotes many Fathers on Baptism of Blood (pp.91-125).

Peter Lombard, *Summa Sententiarum*, Lib.4, Dist.4, N.4, P.L. 192, 847*sq*.

PP Cl. Marc et Fr.X. Gestermann, *Institutiones Morales Alphonsianae*, Tr.2, C.1, A.1 (Paris, 1927), pp.35, 36.

Merkelbach, O.P., *Summa Theologiae Moralis*, T.3 (Paris, 1936), pp.112, 113.

Noldin, S.J., *Summa Theologiae Moralis*, "De Sacramentis," T.3, l.2, Q. 1, No.54-56 (Ratisbone, 1914), pp.62-64.

Dr. Ludwig Ott, *Fundamentals of Catholic Dogma* (T.A.N., 1974), pp.356, 357. He considers the existence of baptism of desire "*sententia fidei proxima.*"

R.P. Thomas Pègues, O.P., *Commentaire français littéral de la Somme Théologique,* XVII, pp.243-250, pp.283-288.

Joannes Perrone, S.J., *Praelectiones Theologicae,* Vol. III (Paris: Gaume Fratres et J. Duprey, 1870), p.96, No.147.

Prümmer, O.P., *Manuale Theologiae Moralis,* T.3, No. 97, 115, 116 (Herder, 1928), pp.90, 91.

Raban Maur, *De Universo,* 4, 10, P.L. 111, 102.

Bishop Scheeben, *Handbuch der katholischen Dogmatik,* §362.

Suarez, *De Sacramentis,* disp. 29.

Tanquerey, *Synopsis theologiae dogmaticae,* T.3, *De Bapt.*, C.3 A.1 (Paris, 1920), pp.286-296.

Tournely, *De Baptismo,* Qu.3, A.1, Concl.2 (Migne, *Cursus theologicus,* 21), p.457.

Zubizarreta, Carm., *Theologia Dogmatica,* (Bilbao, 1939), pp.139-148.

See also the article *Verbum,*[171] No.24 (Winter 1986-1987), in *The Angelus,*[172] June 1989.

---

[171] Available from St. Thomas Aquinas Seminary, RR1, Box 97A-1, Winona, MN 55987.

[172] Available from Angelus Press, 2918 Tracy Ave., Kansas City, MO 64109.

INDEX

Alban, Saint, 55, 57
Albert the Great, Saint, 69, 77
Ambrose, Saint, 24, 42-43, 61-62, 88
Aquinas, Saint Thomas, 12, 21, 42, 89, 105; baptism of desire, 7-8, 9, 69-75; deferral of baptism, 47-49; Eucharist, 38-39, 99n141; necessity of baptism, 34-35, 112; sacraments, 94; salvation, 20, 38-39; sanctifying grace, 92; use of reason, 22, 113-14
Augustine, Saint, 27, 42-43, 79, 88, 102; baptism of blood and of desire, 62-64; baptism of desire, 24; deferral of baptism, 65; necessity of baptism, 34, 37; quoted, 76, 112; salvation, 109n161; unity of Church, 107n156
Augustine Marie of the Blessed Sacrament, 84-85, 104
Baltimore Catechism, 113
baptism, 41, 58n84, 70-72; of blood, 9-10, 66n97, 72-73; character of, 70, 92-98, 108; of desire, 7-8, 18-20
Bede, Saint, 55, 57
Bellarmine, Saint Robert, 60, 89; on the Church, 75-77, 93, 108; quoted, 83
Benedict XV, 32, 54
Bernard, Saint, 24, 63n93, 67-69
Billot, Ludovicus, 79
Billuart, Charles, 36, 83
Bonaventure, Saint, 42, 69
Boniface VIII, 42, 44-45, 97, 111
Borromeo, Saint Charles, 89
Bosco, Saint John, 78
Brownson, Orestes, 81, 83

Canon Law, 32, 89
Canutes, 85
Catherine of Siena, Saint, 78
charity, 106-7, 113
Chrysostom, Saint John, 57
Clement XI, 20
Cohen, Hermann, 84-85, 104
Cornelius a Lapide, 34, 79
Council of Florence, 42, 45-49, 60
Council of Orange, 17-18
Council of Trent, 7, 33, 34, 38, 97; baptism of desire, 49-51; canons on baptism, 88-89, 99n144; catechism, 12, 32, 78; justification, 22-23, 77, 98, 100, 101
Cushing, Richard, 112-15
Cyprian, Saint, 24, 46n61, 57-60, 63, 91
Cyril of Jerusalem, Saint, 57
Damascene, Saint John, 77
Eucharist and salvation, 38-39
Eugene IV, 42, 45-49
Extreme Unction, 99n143
Feeney, Leonard: desire to improve upon the Doctors, 85-86, 92, 111, 115; error of, 91-92, 110-12; excommunication of, 112; Liberals, 15
Fourth Lateran Council, 42-44
Francis, Brother, Open Letter to, 88-89
Franzelin, Johann Baptist, 80
Fulgentius, Saint, 45-47, 60
Garrigou-Lagrange, Reginald, 80-81
Guillemant, Léonie, 84-85
Hay, George, 81
heresies, 16, 42, 65
Hugh of Saint Victor, 67-69, 78

humility, 102
Hutchinson, Thomas A., 46n61
Immaculate Conception, 11
infallibility, 42, 51-52, 87
Innocent III, 10, 42-44, 61, 77, 97, 112
Jacobites, 47
Jerome, Saint, 41, 77
Job, 23–24
John the Baptist, Saint, 102
Jubaianus, 58–59
justice, fulfilled and unfulfilled, 101–3
justification, 22, 54, 96, 98-101, 109
Laisney, François, 98, 107
Leo the Great, Saint, 18, 48
Liguori, Saint Alphonsus, 49, 77, 89
limbo, 66, 114
magisterium of Church, 32, 87, 104-5
Malone, Michael, 87
Martina, Saint, 55
martyrdom, 9-10, 66n97, 72-73
Mary, 29, 37-38
Michael, Brother, 85-86
miracles, 103-4
Müller, Michael, 81-83
mystery, 59n85
Mystici Corporis (Pius XII), 30, 53, 75–76
Nazianzen, Saint Gregory, 57, 64-67
necessity, different forms of, 50, 75n103, 110
Nicholas de Flüe, Saint, 40
Origen, 46n61
original sin, 96, 102
Paul, Saint, 17, 41, 96; on ignorance, 16, 26; on salvation, 21, 28–29
Paulinus of Nola, Saint, 56
Perrone, Joannes, 83
Pius IX, 21, 51-53
Pius X, Saint, 32, 53-54, 89

Pius XII, 29, 30, 80; definition of Church, 75-76; excommunication of Fr. Feeney, 112; ideas taken from others, 53, 79n112
Protestants, inability to be saved, 114-15
Rahner, Karl, 18
re aut voto, 33, 35, 36, 49, 75n103; vs. *in re*, 80, 83; sanctifying grace, 98, 110
rebaptism, 57-58
res sacramenti, 38
Ribadénéira, Father, 55-56
Robert Mary, Brother 36, 53, 56n78, 99; necessity of baptism, 98, 108n160, 109n162; on sacramental character, 95, 107; validity of baptism, 97
Rulleau, Jean-Marc, 88
sacraments, 62n91, 93; exterior sign, 9-10, 26-27; necessity of, 37
salvation, 54, 73-75, 98-101
sanctifying grace, 12-13, 92-98, 108n160, 110
Scripture, interpretation of, 32, 33
Sheen, Fulton, 24-25
Stephen, Pope Saint, 57-58
Summa Theologica (Aquinas), 7-8, 38-39, 47-49, 70-75, 94
Tertullian, 56
unity of Church, 41, 106, 107n156
Valentinian II, 61-62
Vatican I, 33, 87, 111
Vatican II, 15, 104
Wathen, James, 111